A Basis of Fellowship

A Basis of Fellowship

Meditations on a Pentecostal Faith

MIKAEL IVASKA

Foreword by Rick Wadholm Jr.

RESOURCE *Publications* • Eugene, Oregon

A BASIS OF FELLOWSHIP
Meditations on a Pentecostal Faith

Copyright © 2025 Mikael Ivaska. All rights reserved. Except for brief quotations in critical publications or reviews, no part of this book may be reproduced in any manner without prior written permission from the publisher. Write: Permissions, Wipf and Stock Publishers, 199 W. 8th Ave., Suite 3, Eugene, OR 97401.

Resource Publications
An Imprint of Wipf and Stock Publishers
199 W. 8th Ave., Suite 3
Eugene, OR 97401

www.wipfandstock.com

PAPERBACK ISBN: 979-8-3852-4623-6
HARDCOVER ISBN: 979-8-3852-4624-3
EBOOK ISBN: 979-8-3852-4625-0

07/02/25

Scripture quotations taken from The Holy Bible, New International Version® NIV® Copyright © 1973, 1978, 1984, 2011 by Biblica, Inc. Used with permission. All rights reserved worldwide.

This book is dedicated to the people of Vashon Island Community Church.

*"The Bible is our all-sufficient rule for faith and practice. This Statement of Fundamental Truths is intended simply as **a basis of fellowship** among us (i.e., that we all speak the same thing, 1 Corinthians 1:10; Acts 2:42). The phraseology employed in this statement is not inspired or contended for, but the truth set forth is held to be essential to a full-gospel ministry. No claim is made that it contains all biblical truth, only that it covers our need as to these fundamental doctrines."*

Preamble, The Assemblies of God General Council Statement of Fundamental Truths (emphasis mine)

Contents

Acknowledgments		ix
Foreword by Rick Wadholm Jr.		xi
Introduction		xv
1.	The Bible	1
2.	The One, True God	5
3.	Jesus	9
4.	Sin	14
5.	Salvation	19
6.	The Ordinances of the Church (Baptism and Communion)	26
7.	The Baptism in the Holy Spirit	32
8.	Speaking in Tongues	38
9.	Sanctification (Holiness)	44
10.	The Church	49
11.	The Ministry	54
12.	Divine Healing	59
13.	The Blessed Hope (The Rapture of the Church)	65
14.	The Millennial Reign of Christ	69
15.	The Final Judgment	73
16.	The New Heavens and Earth	78

Acknowledgments

TIME AND AGAIN I have read that no book is the product of a single individual. With the completion of this book, I finally understand just how true that statement is.

I have dedicated this book to the people of Vashon Island Community Church, because they deserve it. Thank you, dear VICC family, for allowing me to be your pastor. Thank you for your patience over the years as I have learned (and continue to learn!) what it means to be a pastor, and what it means to preach God's Word.

I would like to thank Daniel Isgrigg of Oral Roberts University for his encouragement on this project, and Rick Wadholm Jr. of the Assemblies of God Theological Seminary for writing the foreword. I would also like to thank Brian Fulthorp, Marty Folsom, Joshua D. Francis, and the many other nerds I've gotten to know over the years in various theology forums on Facebook and elsewhere (the latest, but not the least, being the Assemblies of God Scholars group!).

Thank you also, Kelly Meyer, for your friendship and encouragement both on this project and beyond. Who knew a comic book nerd, former professor of German, lapsed-Pentecostal-turned-adult-convert-to-Roman-Catholicism, was just the sounding board this book needed?!

Thank you, big brother Erik, for your feedback and editing expertise, and to his wife (my sister-in-law) Jess, for sharing him with me.

Thank you, also, to the folks at Wipf & Stock for giving me an opportunity by publishing this book. I hope somebody reads it.

ACKNOWLEDGMENTS

Thank you, Nichole my dear wife, for being such an amazing encouragement. You have believed in me when I haven't believed in myself, and the fact that you continue to do so still amazes me. And to my dear daughter, Ava, for the joy you bring to life. Thanks for putting up with your old man, which can't be very easy, and for finding my dad-jokes as cringy as I find them hilarious.

Thank you, mom and dad. Even though you're in heaven now, and maybe didn't get to see me write this book (though who knows how that works?!), I know you're proud of me.

And last of all: thank you, Living God (Father, Son, and Holy Spirit) for the chance to preach these sermons and to turn them into this book; for the chance to be a husband, a father, a brother, a friend, and a pastor; for the gift of life; and above all, for the gift of life with you. Amen.

Foreword

Sadly, theology has gotten a bad reputation in much of the church.

There are those who say they love theology. They might be obsessed with minutia and looking for a fight to fix all the errors in others because they care so deeply about proper theology (or at least their ideas of such). There are those who say theology is unnecessary. Just love God and neighbor and call it all good. Others may think that doing theology is only really for pastors and Bible scholars, but common folks shouldn't be bothered by such trivialities that don't matter for daily life. Still others may think it matters to give careful thought and evaluation to theological matters but may not be able to put their finger on where theological truths play out in daily life—belief matters for them, but practicality seems hard to come by in theology.

At a basic level, we might consider that we've insufficiently thought about what theology *is* exactly and, thus, may fail to appreciate why it matters or why it *should* matter. Theology isn't boring or trivial (though depending on how we definite it, it definitely can be both).

Understanding theology matters. Living theology matters. Theology matters.

While many would offer that theology is talk *about* or study *of* God (that is its etymology, after all), this simply falls short of what makes for *good* theology and, therefore, what theology properly refers to.

Theology, at its most basic, *is responding well to God's self-revelation*. It is answering the God who has already spoken. . .who has already given himself. It isn't simply talk *about* God. It isn't simply study *of* God. Those are true enough, but they don't get to what theology is fundamentally. Theology is responding to this God as the one revealed in Scripture as the God of Israel, as Father, Son, and Holy Spirit heard in the faithful witnesses of those same Scriptures and confessed by the Church throughout the ages. Theologizing is an act of faith. It is an act of faithfulness.

Again, theology is not simply talking about God. It is the kind of God-talk that takes seriously *this* God's self-revelation.

This God is the one who made the heavens and the earth, the visible and the invisible...and it was good. He is the one who chose a people for himself and made covenant with them to be their God and them to be his people. He is the God who gave himself to and for this people, Israel, not because of who they were but because of who he is. He is the God who chose Israel not for their sake, but for the sake of the whole world. He is the God overshadowing the virgin. The God met in the man from Nazareth—Jesus—crucified, died, buried, resurrected on the third day, ascended to heaven, and coming again to judge the living and the dead. He is the God richly poured out on sons and daughters from the Day of Pentecost to our own day, bearing witness to King Jesus as God's plan to set all things to rights.

If *this* is *that* God...then what kind of practice of theology is the right way to do theology?

Let me offer a few of the ways found in Scripture and to which this book will take up.

Theology is prayer. It is worship. It is faithful witness in word and deed. It is practicing the life of the Spirit that fills to overflowing. It is making holy. It is healing. It is cleansing and delivering from the chaos of rebellion against the very life of God. It is the forgiveness of sins and newness of life now and yet to come. It is life in community for the sake of others where we confess in word and deed *this* God—who he is, what he has done, what he is doing, and what he will do.

Thus, to practice theology well is to respond appropriately to God's self-giving as Father, Son, and Holy Spirit. It is to live as the people of God as witness to the life of God.

Having said all of this, what you now hold in your hands is a book taking up this simple (not simplistic) idea of theology. It isn't a book meant to unpack theology in depth. It is a book meant to offer one pastor and one congregation's hearing of God's self-revelation (as confessed in a particular church's theology) and seek to faithfully respond. It is a book seeking to take seriously the theology of one church (the Assemblies of God) as a call to live faithfully before God. It isn't meant as a rejection of other church statements of faith, but only to take seriously *this* church's theological statement.

The kind of theology this book offers is not a wrestling at length with the nuances of the "Statement of Fundamental Truths" of the Assemblies of God (USA). That can be found in a number of other books. Instead, here is offered a mature pastoral preaching of the messages within this "Statement," offered in the vein of a Eugene Peterson or a Frederick Buechner for their own congregational contexts (witty, insightful, fun, provocative, stirring).

As a series of sermons turned into a book this doesn't mean you will read "three points and a poem" in what follows (a terrible model of preaching from a bygone era). Talk about making a boring book to read. Instead, it means you will be invited to join the 2024 Assemblies of God congregation of Vashon Island, Washington, in hearing the words of their pastor, Mike Ivaska.

Mike gives voice to faithful living *into* and *out of* this "Statement." This isn't meant that the "Statement" is in any way intended as an end-all of what can and must be said faithfully in theology (it isn't, and Mike makes that clear), but only that good theology is lived theology. And as a lived theology, Mike feels the burden of offering it up for a real community of those invited to follow Jesus.

The theology you have taken up to read is offered in a storied sermonic fashion meant to envision ways of living into theological statements far too often removed from the life of those who confess them. It is offered as the confession of a particular church (and we are all meant to belong to such communities). It is offered as a series of sermons of Scripture that are organized according to the "Statement" of that particular congregation. It is offered as a prolonged prayer seeking to answer the living Word of the Living God in faithfulness in the very context Mike (and his congregation) lives.

In this way, it is offered to a wider readership to seek for us to hear (along with them) and live faithfully into God's self-revelation. Having heard the Lord speaking, how should we answer?

Again, this is not everything that must be said, but it is a great start to a journey meant for all who likewise claim this Fellowship as their Fellowship.

To those who have found themselves journeying with the Assemblies of God (USA), you will find in this book a brief but faithful testimony to live into what you have confessed along the way. And in hearing these messages, may we all grow in our lived love of Jesus: Savior, Healer, Baptizer in the Spirit, and Soon-Coming King! Amen and amen!

RICK WADHOLM, JR.
Associate Professor of Old Testament
Assemblies of God Theological Seminary

Introduction

LIKE MANY OTHER PEOPLE, I've had fantasies about being someone (or something) other than what I am for much of my life. When I was a kid, I thought I'd be a jet pilot when I grew up. In middle school, I considered (but never attempted) standup comedy. By high school, I was certain my future was to be a professional bass player in a rock-reggae band. With the exception of an unpaid six months in said rock-reggae band, none of these fantasies ever quite worked out.

This tendency toward fantasy, it seems, doesn't go away after we become adults. At least, it didn't for me. Now that I'm a pastor, my primary fantasy has been (on and off for twenty years) to be a theologian and a scholar. Because of this fantasy, there was a time (in my head, if nowhere else) when this book was going to be a profound theological tome—a mighty exposition of the Assemblies of God's *Statement of Fundamental Truths*. But scholar I am not, professional theologian I am not (beyond what goes into being a pastor), and therefore "tome" this—alas—has not turned out to be.

God has given the church many gifts, and sometimes we pastors can overestimate the significance of our own. Jesus needs moms, dads, kids, teachers, students, grocery clerks, and garbage men, too. He needs every different kind of person he has made if his church is going to be the church he intends it to be: salt and light, flavoring and enlightening every nook and cranny of God's green earth. The role of pastor is just one tiny part of that whole. Nevertheless, we pastors do have a few important tasks within the Christian community. As the name implies, our job is to be a shepherd, or gentle guide. We do this in conversation and relationship. We do this in providing leadership to the communities under our care. And we also do this in our preaching and teaching.

The book you hold in your hand is the record of about four months of preaching, during which time I took my congregation through our denomination's statement of faith. As with all preaching, it is at times very context-specific. So what is that context?

I am pastor to a small church of about 40 folks on an island of about ten-thousand people. Unlike most small towns in America, our community is primarily wealthy, well-educated, and highly progressive. Churches in our town are not large. There is only one church (possibly two) that breaks 100 in attendance each week. All churches combined (liberal, conservative, Catholic, Protestant, Orthodox, etc.) make up ten percent or less of the island's population. The folks who come to my church come because it's a place where they can follow Jesus and be taught out of the Bible. With the exception of those who invest time and ferry fare into worshipping on the mainland each week (or, what's worse, just go to church online), there is very little freedom for islanders to pick the church whose theology and practice is "just so."

The people with whom I worship on Sunday could generally care less what denomination I represent. Nevertheless, our statement of faith (the Assemblies of God *Statement of Fundamental Truths*) is the doctrinal plumb line of our congregation. Because of this dynamic, you will notice that when I walk through our statement with my people, my goal is always to bring them together rather than to draw lines between them. There are certain points the reader may wish I emphasized differently. Perhaps this small recognition of my situation (a representative of a particular theological tradition pastoring a congregation who is not necessarily gathered together for the sake of that tradition) can be helpful to you.

You'll also notice that, as with all sermons in all churches everywhere, these sermons took place in the context of actual, lived life. Two deaths in our larger church and island community took place during this series. I picked up a part time job at the grocery

INTRODUCTION

store where my wife works. The last five sermons overlapped with the Advent-Christmas season. It's these contextual facts that, I believe, make these sermons worth reading—not because of my expert handling of text and topic, but because these sermons give the reader a chance to see belief working itself out in real life. It's less important to me that the reader believe every point of Pentecostal doctrine (or agree with my handling of it) than it is she or he come along with me for the ride. As will hopefully become obvious in the reading, my goal for my people was something similar.

There is a long history in the church of publishing sermons for the edification and education of God's people. And while I hesitate to class the sermons in this book alongside the works of John Wesley, John Calvin, or Saint Augustine (for they would obviously fall far short), these sermons could perhaps be read as something like the Pentecostal version of the work of Frederick Buechner (though I would also hesitate to rank my sermons with his). If my philosophy for these sermons could be articulated, it would be "apologetics through witness." I was trying to show my people the value of a thought by expressing what it's like to believe in that thought.

And finally, a warning to the reader: My sermons tend to be quite brief, especially by Pentecostal standards, and in this series I neither define nor defend any doctrinal point in too great of detail. The scripture passages I quote are as much a part of the sermons as anything I myself happened to write. I expected my people to listen to them and not treat them like the opening credits to the main event of the sermon. Likewise, I hope the reader will read them and not rush past them to see what *I* have to say. I once read that theologian Karl Barth didn't think a sermon should be recorded and put on a record unless the entire service was recorded and put on the record, too. I guess my desire is similar to his in that I want you, the reader, to (as much as possible) experience these chapters as sermons set in the context of worship. Reading meditatively over the scripture passage would go a long way toward making that happen.

INTRODUCTION

For a more official exposition of the Assemblies of God statement of faith, I would direct the reader to *Bible Doctrines: A Pentecostal Perspective* by William Menzies and Stanley Horton. For something more academic, I would direct people to the systematic theologies of Frank Macchia and Amos Yong. And if, for some reason, you wanted to know my own favorite compendium of Pentecostal Christian belief, it would be the almost century-old book, *Knowing the Doctrines of the Bible* by Myer Pearlman. It's a good one and you should read it.

And lastly, of course, if you want to read the entire Assemblies of God *Statement of Fundamental Truths* for yourself, you can do that by just googling it and following the link.

1.

The Bible

10 You, however, know all about my teaching, my way of life, my purpose, faith, patience, love, endurance, **11** persecutions, sufferings—what kinds of things happened to me in Antioch, Iconium and Lystra, the persecutions I endured. Yet the Lord rescued me from all of them. **12** In fact, everyone who wants to live a godly life in Christ Jesus will be persecuted, **13** while evildoers and impostors will go from bad to worse, deceiving and being deceived. **14** But as for you, continue in what you have learned and have become convinced of, because you know those from whom you learned it, **15** and how from infancy you have known the Holy Scriptures, which are able to make you wise for salvation through faith in Christ Jesus. **16** All Scripture is God-breathed and is useful for teaching, rebuking, correcting and training in righteousness, **17** so that the servant of God may be thoroughly equipped for every good work.

4:1 In the presence of God and of Christ Jesus, who will judge the living and the dead, and in view of his appearing and his kingdom, I give you this charge: **2** Preach the word; be prepared in season and out of season; correct, rebuke and encourage—with great patience and careful instruction. **3** For the time will come when people will not put up with sound doctrine. Instead, to suit their own desires, they will gather around them a great number of teachers to say

A BASIS OF FELLOWSHIP

what their itching ears want to hear. **4** *They will turn their ears away from the truth and turn aside to myths.* **5** *But you, keep your head in all situations, endure hardship, do the work of an evangelist, discharge all the duties of your ministry.*

2 Timothy 3:10—4:5

WHEN I WAS A kid, I thought my dad was physically incapable of giving short answers. I'd ask him a yes or no question and he'd go into a story about his cousin. I'd ask permission to do something and he'd tell me about some time he did something similar, and how that turned out for him. I knew never to ask his opinion on a topic unless I had time to spare and nowhere to go. By the time I was a teenager, I began asking my dad to answer the question *first*, and *then* he could tell me the story. Usually, he would just chuckle as a whole new story came to mind.

I suppose one theory for why my dad answered questions like this is that he was a preacher. He talked for a living, so maybe when he got home, he just couldn't stop. But that's not quite true. With a hot cup of coffee and a newspaper, my dad could sit in silence for what felt like hours. He'd call it "recharging his battery." No, dad didn't need to talk just to talk. As I think back on it, I think my dad told me stories whenever I was looking for answers because he believed the answers were in the stories themselves. And if we were good listeners, we'd hear it.

I want to spend the rest of this year going through our church's statement of faith. As an Assemblies of God-affiliated congregation, the doctrinal framework of our church comes from a century-old document called *The Statement of Fundamental Truths*. We won't go through the document word for word, but mainly just through the topics the document raises. This is going to provide for all of us either an introduction to basic Christian doctrine, or a refresher course. In the latter half of the series (or so), some of the doctrinal distinctives of our fellowship will come up—such as our belief in divine healing or spiritual gifts like speaking in tongues. Our by-laws as a congregation allow a lot of freedom on these secondary doctrinal issues, and so my handling of these topics will not be divisive (I hope!). But most of our statement of faith, especially the first several points, contains basic Christian positions held by all historic evangelicals, and most of them by all Christians of whatever stripe. The first doctrinal point in our statement of faith is on our understanding of the Bible, and it reads like this:

> *"The Scriptures, both the Old and New Testaments, are verbally inspired of God and are the revelation of God to man, the infallible, authoritative rule of faith and conduct."*

In our passage this morning from 2 Timothy, an aged apostle Paul is writing to his young and timid protégé, Timothy. Timothy is the son of a Jewish mother and a Greek father, and there is reason to believe his relationship to his father is estranged. As a young man, Timothy joined Paul's missionary team, and now a few years later Paul has placed Timothy in charge of the congregation at Ephesus. Paul is in prison and appears not to expect to live much longer. The church in Ephesus has been dealing with false teaching and sin. Because of this, Timothy has established new leadership in the church and will hopefully be able to come to Paul soon. But until then, Paul says in our text, Timothy has a job to do: *preach the word.*

In verses 10 and 11, Paul reminds Timothy of Paul's own suffering for the gospel, and in 12 and 13, Paul reminds Timothy that suffering is in fact part of life if we want to stay faithful to Jesus. Further down, in the first five verses of chapter 4, Paul exhorts Timothy to faithfulness in his task, and to resist being the sort of teacher who simply tells people what they want to hear. But in the middle of our text, in chapter 3, verses 14 to 17, Paul tells Timothy where Timothy is going to find guidance and strength: in the word of God written.

From his mother's knee, Paul says, Timothy has known the Jewish Scriptures (our Old Testament). And now that he has come to faith in Jesus of Nazareth, Israel's Messiah, he understands these Scriptures even more—not only as the record of his people and the laws of his nation, but as a word of promise and hope that finds its culmination of Jesus. These Scriptures, Paul says, are God-breathed, the work of God's Spirit, a faithful and reliable witness from God for the church. They will be the tool in Timothy's hand and the source of his teaching.

For us as Christians today, of course, the Scriptures have grown to include the New Testament, which in Paul and Timothy's day was literally being written. The Jesus who fulfills Israel's hope, and the apostles who planted the church, speak to us today in the Gospels and letters of the New Testament. The Spirit has given us the Bible, Old Testament and New, that we might know Jesus. It's God's word to us, as a community and as individuals. It's our source of truth, inspiration, and guidance. And that makes me think of my dad.

When we come to the Bible looking for answers, what we find more often than not is a story. Sure, there are letters, such as we're reading today. And there are laws, and poems, and proverbs. But for the most part, the Bible is story. Even the parts that aren't story don't make too much sense if divorced from the story. We come to the Bible wanting answers, and God starts telling us a story.

As we go through our statement of faith for the next few months, my hope is that we all get more established in sound doctrine, more united and understanding of our theology, and more able to wrestle with things about which we might not agree. But I will have failed if this series makes you think of the Bible as a poorly organized encyclopedia of facts, as a dictionary made by someone who can't get to the point, or if I make myself appear as the expert finder-of-doctrinal-information.

The Bible is God's word to the church, "our all-sufficient rule for faith and practice," as it says in the preamble to our statement of faith. But the Bible, above all, is a story—in particular, the story of Jesus—and it's *stories* our Father primarily wants to tell.

Let's Pray

2.

The One, True God

> 9 *At that time Jesus came from Nazareth in Galilee and was baptized by John in the Jordan.* 10 *Just as Jesus was coming up out of the water, he saw heaven being torn open and the Spirit descending on him like a dove.* 11 *And a voice came from heaven: "You are my Son, whom I love; with you I am well pleased."*
>
> Mark 1:9-11

DO YOU REMEMBER THE days of VHS tapes and video rental stores? I always groaned as a kid when adults would wax romantic about their childhood and adolescent years in the 1950's and 60's, but now I look back on life in the 80's and 90's the same way. And few things bear such a golden glow of 90's nostalgia like Friday nights at the video rental store.

Every Friday night, my dad would bring my brother and I uptown. He would drop us off at the video store and head off to order a pizza. My brother would always pick out a comedy, and I would pick out an action movie—preferably something with Arnold Schwarzenegger or Godzilla in it. Dad would come back, pick out a movie for him and mom, and back home we'd go. Because I was the younger brother, we always watched my older brother Erik's movie first. (Generally, I had to wait to watch my movie sometime

A BASIS OF FELLOWSHIP

Saturday before they were due back.) Friday night was always pizza and a movie before our slightly-later-than-weeknight bedtime. When we were older, we watched our movies on our own, on the second TV downstairs.

One of the movies my brother rented once was *Nuns on the Run*. If my dad had been running more effective interference, he would've stopped us from renting this particular film. But he didn't, so we watched it. And at our age, we probably didn't need to see all the things we saw in that movie. But besides the less-than-age-appropriate material in the movie, one scene in particular stands out to me for its profound theological content (or not, as the case may be).

Nuns on the Run is a corny 90's comedy starring Eric Idle of *Monty Python* fame. He and another British comedian, Robbie Coltrane, play two crooks on the run from both the cops and their own crime boss. To escape being arrested or killed, they hide in a local convent and pretend to be nuns. Robbie Coltrane's character has a Catholic background, but Eric Idle's does not. The convent in which the two men pretend to be nuns is connected to a Catholic girls' high school, and Eric Idle's character is assigned the task of teaching the religion class. The first class, of course, is on the Trinity.

Remembering his days learning the catechism, Robbie Coltrane tries to explain to Idle how the Trinity works, eventually falling upon Saint Patrick's famous analogy of the shamrock: the shamrock is one flower made of three leaves. It is one, and it is also three. It is three, but it is also one. When it comes time for Idle to explain the Trinity to his students, he panics and exclaims, "The Trinity is like a shamrock: small, green, and split three ways!"

The second fundamental truth in our statement of faith reads, in part:

> "The one true God has revealed himself as the eternally self-existent 'I AM' the Creator of heaven and earth and the Redeemer of mankind. He has further revealed himself as embodying the principles of relationship and association as Father, Son, and Holy Spirit."

The Bible never attempts to convince anyone of the existence of God. The knowledge of God is assumed, and anyone who denies the divine reality is labeled in Scripture a "fool." God, rather than being argued for, is simply *there*: the ground and source of all that is. Whereas in our day the struggle is often with doubt about God's existence, the biblical writers are far more concerned with idolatry, or false understandings of God.

In the Old Testament, most nations had their own tribal deities. There were also gods who were tied to particular places and gods who ruled over particular realities, like fertility or the weather. By New Testament times, the great pantheons were starting to be identified with one another. The Greek Zeus was the Roman Jupiter; the Roman Venus was the Greek Aphrodite. Religions and spiritualities from the East also entered the Roman and Middle Eastern world: Zoroastrianism, with its dualistic understanding, and even Buddhism, with its lack of a personal god.

Against all this, the Jewish people (including the authors of Scripture) held out belief in one God, the God who had chosen them—the God of Abraham, Isaac, and Jacob. This God was the maker of heaven and earth, and beside him there were no gods. Certainly, the earliest Israelites may have come to this realization slowly, and backsliding into the worship of many gods was a constant temptation. But by the close of the Old Testament, the conclusion was clear: the God of Israel is the one true God; the idols of the nations are nothing, and any spiritual reality behind them (aside from the superstitions of their worshipers) are realities that oppose themselves to God and mean humanity no good. It was in the context of this conviction (that there is only one God) that Jesus of Nazareth came.

Jesus came to the Jewish people to reveal God as Father, and he told his disciples that to see him was to see the Father. In Jesus, the first disciples found healing, forgiveness, and redemption. Through Jesus, they learned to relate to their Maker not only as King but as Parent. They experienced the divine in a way no one had experienced it before. And, especially after the resurrection, they came to the conviction that in and through Jesus they had more deeply come to know God. At Pentecost, with the outpouring of the Holy Spirit, they again experienced God in a radical new way. God was not just above, or in the face of Jesus, but living inside them as well. God was Father. God was Jesus. And God was Holy Spirit. The Christian doctrine of the Trinity was, and is, born of the new reality revealed by Christ, the fruit of revelation and experience.

Sometimes, like for Eric Idle in *Nuns on the Run*, the Trinity can strike us as a nonsensical mystery or an unsolvable riddle. And, at first, the language of the church doesn't seem to help: *one essence, three persons; one God, three times*. But the church's theologizing about the Trinity is there, really, to preserve the mystery. While heretics take apart the Trinity—often in the name of logic and reason, grabbing one truth or one Scripture to the neglect of others—believers adore the Trinity. It overwhelms our faculties, rings true to Scripture, guides our experience, and preserves both the unity and plurality within God.

The God who made us is thrice personal. The God who made us is, therefore, love. He who made us is himself relationship and communion. The God who made us is Father, Son, and Holy Spirit—one in three, and three in one.

Today, as we dwell upon the mystery of God, let's enjoy the fact that our very faith bears a trinitarian shape, as the Father reaches out to us through the Son by the power of the Spirit, and we in the Spirit come to Jesus who brings us back to the Father.

Let's Pray

3.

Jesus

3 *Praise be to the God and Father of our Lord Jesus Christ, who has blessed us in the heavenly realms with every spiritual blessing in Christ.* **4** *For he chose us in him before the creation of the world to be holy and blameless in his sight. In love* **5** *he predestined us for adoption to sonship through Jesus Christ, in accordance with his pleasure and will—* **6** *to the praise of his glorious grace, which he has freely given us in the One he loves.* **7** *In him we have redemption through his blood, the forgiveness of sins, in accordance with the riches of God's grace* **8** *that he lavished on us. With all wisdom and understanding,* **9** *he made known to us the mystery of his will according to his good pleasure, which he purposed in Christ,* **10** *to be put into effect when the times reach their fulfillment—to bring unity to all things in heaven and on earth under Christ.*

11 *In him we were also chosen, having been predestined according to the plan of him who works out everything in conformity with the purpose of his will,* **12** *in order that we, who were the first to put our hope in Christ, might be for the praise of his glory.* **13** *And you also were included in Christ when you heard the message of truth, the gospel of your salvation. When you believed, you were marked in him with a seal, the promised Holy Spirit,* **14** *who is a*

A BASIS OF FELLOWSHIP

deposit guaranteeing our inheritance until the redemption of those who are God's possession—to the praise of his glory.

Ephesians 1:3–14

JESUS IS THE CENTER of our faith. We're so aware of this that it feels like a cliché to say it. But it's true. There really is no Christianity without Jesus. There's no New Testament without Jesus. There's no church without Jesus. There's no Trinity, or at least no revelation of the Trinity, without Jesus. There's no understanding of salvation by grace through faith without Jesus. There's no real reason to believe in life after death without Jesus. There's certainly no reason to believe in resurrection without Jesus. Some have even said there is no reason to believe in God without Jesus.

Just a few months ago, on June 3rd of this year, an important German theologian named Jürgen Moltmann passed away. Dr. Moltmann wrote many books and mentored many people, including my friend Bjørn, one of the local Lutheran church's former pastors. I never had the chance to meet Dr. Moltmann, but I literally only missed him by a matter of months. Around the time I became youth pastor here (about twenty years ago), I went to hear Dr. Moltmann give a lecture at Seattle Pacific University. A few months later, I made the rounds here on Vashon, trying to get to know some of the other local pastors. This was when I met my friend Bjørn (a German-born Lutheran who had emigrated to America with his American wife, Lynn), only to find out, years later, that when Moltmann had been in Seattle giving that lecture I heard, he was staying at Bjørn's house here on Vashon. If I had met Bjørn just a little bit earlier, I may have wound up eating barbecue with arguably the most important theologian of my lifetime.

Jürgen Moltmann came to faith in a prisoner of war camp in Great Britain following the second world war. He had been raised in an unbelieving German family and served as a Hitler Youth. He and some of his friends had been assigned to the antiaircraft guns when the Allies firebombed the German city of Dresden. His friends were killed right in front of him, he himself only narrowly escaping with his life. When he was transferred to an infantry unit and sent to defend the homeland against the advancing British, he determined then and there to surrender the first chance he got. After some harrowing encounters, he finally found the opportunity. He threw down his rifle at the feet of a British soldier and surrendered to him in the best English he could manage.

In his memoir, Dr. Moltmann describes the utter shame and disillusion he and his fellow Germans felt after the war. He also describes his surprise, as a prisoner of war, at how kindly he was treated by his captors, both while still on the continent and then after being transferred to Great Britain. He and his fellow prisoners were given food and offered the chance to take classes. Because of the devout faith of many in Great Britain and America at that time, he and his fellow prisoners were also witnessed to and offered Bibles. Though not a believer, Moltmann accepted a Bible and began reading it. He soon found himself relating strongly to the words of despair and abandonment in some of the psalms, and to the biblical picture of Jesus as "a man of sorrows and acquainted with grief." In coming to identify with this figure of the abandoned and rejected Jesus, he became a believer. He would eventually return to Germany and become a pastor, then a professor, and then the author of some of the 20th century's most groundbreaking theological works. Decades later, in a video interview with one of his former students, Dr. Moltmann would put it this way: "Without Jesus, I would not believe in God. Without Jesus, I would be an atheist."

The third article in our statement of faith reads like this:

> "The Lord Jesus Christ is the eternal Son of God. The Scriptures declare: His virgin birth, his sinless life, his miracles, his substitutionary work on the cross, his bodily resurrection from the dead, [and] his exaltation to the right hand of God."

In other words, Jesus is the one who brings us God, who shows us God, who is God walking among us in human flesh. He entered our world in a special way through the womb of his mother, Mary. He lived in perfect harmony and obedience to his heavenly Father. He healed the sick, comforted the hurting, and even raised some from the dead. When he went to the cross, he identified himself with a world of sin and cried out to his Father, "Eloi, eloi! Lama sabachthani?" "My God, my God, why have you forsaken me?" (This, incidentally, is the image of Jesus that spoke so savingly to Dr. Moltmann.). After taking the sin of the world upon himself at the cross, Jesus rose again from the grave, never to die again. And having ascended into heaven, he now sits at the right hand of God the Father, from whence he will come to judge the living and the dead.

In our passage this morning, the apostle Paul reflects on the wonderful centrality of Jesus in our relationship with God. "Praise be to the God and Father of our Lord Jesus Christ," Paul says. Every spiritual blessing, every grace we know, is given to us in Jesus. Sending Jesus into this world was God's way of choosing us. Before the foundation of the world, God had intended to send his son. Heaven and earth would be made one in him. From eternity past, it was always God's plan to bring heaven and earth together through the incarnation of his Son. When sin got in the way, Jesus atoned for us at the cross. He purchased our forgiveness and redeemed us with his blood. Through Jesus, God has shown us God's ultimate purpose: unity and peace. And by faith in Jesus, God has sealed us for eternity and given us the Holy Spirit.

Jesus is the center of our faith. He is the center of God's plan. He is the Lord and King of his church, and the Savior of this lost world. To look into Jesus' face is to see God. To look at his relation to the Father, and his dependence on the Spirit, is to see that God is triune—three in one and one in three. To look at Jesus is to see not just *hope* that God is love, but the *revelation* that God is love—that even sin and death can't separate us from God, because, in Jesus, God has conquered sin and death.

I know some people who would rather not call themselves Christians and would rather call themselves followers of Jesus. "Christian," they say, carries too much cultural and historical baggage. They are just simple followers of Jesus. I get what they're saying, and sometimes that's the terminology I use for myself, too. But Jesus isn't just someone we follow. He's also someone who has saved us. He is the face of God to us. He is the ground and source of our lives. More than mere followers of Jesus, we Christians are worshippers of Jesus. He is our salvation. And he is our life.

Let's Pray

4.

Sin

13 *When tempted, no one should say, "God is tempting me." For God cannot be tempted by evil, nor does he tempt anyone;* **14** *but each person is tempted when they are dragged away by their own evil desire and enticed.* **15** *Then, after desire has conceived, it gives birth to sin; and sin, when it is full-grown, gives birth to death.*

James 1:13–15

IT'S BEEN SAID THAT the Christian doctrine of original sin (or the universal sinfulness of humanity) is the only Christian doctrine that can be empirically verified. We humans are a strange mixture of goodness and badness, selfishness and generosity. And sometimes the apparently good and generous among us turn out to be the worst.

For a while, I became fascinated by combat footage from the Ukraine war, mainly because there is simply so much of it. Thanks to cellphones, drones, and Go-Pro cameras, the Ukraine war is the most heavily video-documented military conflict in human history. There is a lot of footage you can watch, though I don't really recommend it. Some of it is fascinating. Some of it is action-packed. Some is heartbreaking. And some is just downright gruesome. It is a war being fought between those who are defending their homeland and those who are far from home and have been told they fight for a noble cause against forces of evil. Both sides believe they are doing right. And both, because such is the nature of war, are absolutely brutal toward their enemies.

In C.S. Lewis's fictional book *The Screwtape Letters*, junior demon Wormwood writes to his more experienced uncle, Screwtape, rejoicing at the outbreak of war. Screwtape corrects him. Yes, war is an opportunity for hatred, suffering, and death. But it's also an opportunity for bravery, sacrifice, and honor. Demon Screwtape warns his nephew that there is as much about war that can play into "the Enemy's" (i.e., God's) hands as into the hands of "Our Father Below" (the devil). By no means has Wormwood's job become easier now that war has broken out. If anything, the demons now have even more work to do.

As the writer of that story, and a veteran of World War One, war was something Lewis could write about with confidence. War is one of humanity's great evils, but it's also a paradoxical (though terrifying) opportunity for much human good. War is when we exercise hate. But peace is when we exercise gluttony. Soldiers, while busy inflicting unimaginable carnage on their enemies, will also, at the drop of a hat, risk their very lives for their friends. Peacetime, though certainly preferable to war, also gives us more opportunity for petty selfishness, laziness, drunkenness, and lust. Certainly, soldiers on leave can live lives of wanton hedonism, but peacetime gives us all the opportunity to be lazy and slothful, lackadaisical sort of hedonists (when we get around to it). War is not so much a source of human evil as an expression of it, and peacetime offers as many opportunities for sin as does war—even if war is something we should never want, and we should always try to avoid.

The fourth Fundamental Truth in our statement of faith is entitled, The Fall of Man, and it reads like this:

> "Man was created good and upright; for God said, "Let us make man in our own image, after our likeness.' However, man by voluntary transgression fell and thereby incurred not only physical death but also spiritual death, which is separation from God."

This, of course, refers to Adam and Eve's sin in the Garden of Eden in Genesis 3. God had created a world that was "very good." He planted a garden for Adam and Eve and placed them in it. As a symbol of his authority, and their limitation, God declared one tree in the garden off limits. The rest they could have. "That one is mine," God basically said, and he called it the Tree of the Knowledge of Good and Evil—probably not because of some magical property in the tree, but because if they ate of its fruit they'd learn what conscience is, and by breaking their consciences, they'd go from only knowing good to knowing evil as well.

If you know the story of the Bible, you know what happens next. The serpent tempts Eve to disbelieve God, to think that God is holding out on her. She believes the serpent, disbelieves God, and plucks some of the fruit. She takes a bite and gives some to Adam. He also takes a bite, and then it happens. Their eyes open to who they are, and to what they are. They see their own nakedness and experience shame for the first time. They hide from God, and when confronted by God, blame God and each other (and the serpent) for what they've done. But God respects them too much for that. Their choices are theirs, so the consequences will be theirs, too. God clothes them and sends them out of the Garden to live off the rocky soil of the earth. No longer can they live in the Garden. No longer can they eat from the Tree of Life. It's the story of the fall of humanity. It's the story of each one of us, and our individual and collective loss of innocence.

In our passage today, James, the half-brother of Jesus, is writing to his fellow Jewish Christians. The book of James may be one of our earliest New Testament letters, though we have no idea the date. The letter itself seems almost like a sermon. It also reads a bit like the book of Proverbs. It's very practical and very blunt, while still carrying an air of poetry and metaphor. Because of its very Jewish character and positive statements about the law, Martin Luther once called it "an epistle of straw" and didn't think it should be in our Bibles. But cooler heads prevailed, and we Protestants can still read James alongside the letters of Paul.

Our passage is concerned with the practical issue of sin. No one, James says, should blame God for the fact that they want to sin. God is good and is, in fact, goodness itself. He cannot be tempted by evil any more than water can be tempted to stop being wet. If something goes dry, it's because the water's been taken out. If water returns, things turn wet once again. In the same way, God and evil are opposites—not opposites of equal power, but opposites of presence and absence. When we want to sin, it's not because God wants us to sin. It's because we're not listening to God. God isn't gone, but we're acting like he is.

Sin, James says, comes from our relationship to our wants. The NIV reads in verse 14, "evil desire," but the translators are just trying to show us a little mercy. The Greek says "desire," and it means "strong desire." It's a word often translated lust, but it's also the word Luke uses to describe the Prodigal Son's desire to eat pig food when he was starving. It's the word used to describe "the lust of the flesh" in 1 John 2:16, but also the "longing" of the Old Testament prophets to see the days of Christ in Matthew 13:17. Our desires are sometimes evil. But sometimes they're just our desires. The problem, James says, is our relationship to those desires. What is it we desire? And what are we willing to do to satisfy our desire?

Temptation, James says, comes from our willingness to entertain a wrong desire, or to entertain a legitimate desire in a wrong sort of way. Most healthy adults have a sex drive, for example, but sex is created for the context of a committed marriage between and a man and a woman. It's not wrong to want sex. It *is* wrong to act on that desire with someone who's not your spouse, or in sex that conflicts with God's design. It's not wrong to be hungry. It's not wrong to defend your homeland. It's not wrong to serve your country. But how are you going to satisfy that hunger? What will you do to defend that homeland? How will you treat those who are not in your group?

As we entertain these desires and contemplate our willingness to do wrong, our desires, James says, give birth to sin. We sin in thought. We sin in deed. We sin in avoiding the right and embracing the wrong. And having set out on the path of sin, we begin a journey that can only lead to death—death to innocence, death to harmony, death to being able to look ourselves and each other in the eye. And, above all, death to God. "In the day you eat of that tree you will die," warned God. Eve and Adam ate of the tree and didn't die. Not exactly. Not immediately. But something important *did* die that day.

In his letter to the Romans, the apostle Paul tells his readers, "The wages of sin is death." We get what we deserve, and to choose the path of sin is to choose to be paid in death. Adam and Eve sinned and passed on that death to all their children. Our parents passed on their sin to us, and we pass on our sin to our kids. Even without having children, we pass on our sin to our neighbors and friends. It's like wet paint on our fingers that puts a little stain on whatever we touch.

"But the free gift of God is eternal life in Christ Jesus," continues Paul. And "eternal" here isn't just duration but quality. If giving ourselves to sin, which we've all done, leads to death, then turning to God through Christ, Paul says, gives us life. By entering into death with us, Jesus has reversed the course of sin and given us back our life. More than that, he has given us *his* life in place of the one we've all given up. Where our sin brings us guilt, Jesus pays our debt. Where our sin feels too powerful, Jesus defeats it. Where our sin separates us from ourselves, Jesus puts us back together. And where our sin separates us from God, Jesus brings us home.

One of the biggest criticisms of the Christian faith is our doctrine of sin. It seems like such a negative view of humanity. But we Christians reply that we're just being realistic. The world, and even our own lives, are too full of examples to deny the reality and destructiveness of sin. But sin isn't the Christian message. It's just the shadow around the bright center of Christ. Whatever guilt, error, addiction, or disobedience there might be in our lives, it is nothing against the power of Christ to redeem. The human experience is sin. The believer's experience is Christ.

Let's Pray

5.

Salvation

3:1 *Now there was a Pharisee, a man named Nicodemus who was a member of the Jewish ruling council.* **2** *He came to Jesus at night and said, "Rabbi, we know that you are a teacher who has come from God. For no one could perform the signs you are doing if God were not with him."*

3 *Jesus replied, "Very truly I tell you, no one can see the kingdom of God unless they are born again."*

4 *"How can someone be born when they are old?" Nicodemus asked. "Surely they cannot enter a second time into their mother's womb to be born!"*

5 *Jesus answered, "Very truly I tell you, no one can enter the kingdom of God unless they are born of water and the Spirit.* **6** *Flesh gives birth to flesh, but the Spirit gives birth to spirit.* **7** *You should not be surprised at my saying, 'You must be born again.'* **8** *The wind blows wherever it pleases. You hear its sound, but you cannot tell where it comes from or where it is going. So it is with everyone born of the Spirit."*

9 *"How can this be?" Nicodemus asked.*

A BASIS OF FELLOWSHIP

> 10 *"You are Israel's teacher," said Jesus, "and do you not understand these things?* 11 *Very truly I tell you, we speak of what we know, and we testify to what we have seen, but still you people do not accept our testimony.* 12 *I have spoken to you of earthly things and you do not believe; how then will you believe if I speak of heavenly things?* 13 *No one has ever gone into heaven except the one who came from heaven—the Son of Man.* 14 *Just as Moses lifted up the snake in the wilderness, so the Son of Man must be lifted up,* 15 *that everyone who believes may have eternal life in him."*

John 3:1–15

I DON'T KNOW IF everyone knows this, but I recently accepted the offer of a part time job. It's something I can do in addition to my work here at the church. One of our local grocery stores (I'll leave it to you to guess which one) needed a fill-in driver one day a week to pick up supplies in the city. Don't worry. Things are going well here at the church. Nichole and I have a few financial goals we're trying to meet. And it seemed like the sort of thing I could pick up without much negative effect on the church or our personal lives. So this past week, I started training to be a driver.

It's amazing how odd it feels, after fifteen years of working here at the church full time, to put on a uniform and punch into an hourly job. At first, I was very self-conscious, afraid people might think I didn't work here at the church anymore. Then I started to realize how much ego goes along with a titled career like "pastor." For some reason, I felt a little "less" being a grocery store delivery driver than being a pastor. I didn't feel the *other* grocery workers were less. I just felt, for some reason, that *I* was. It was a real revelation of the pride that has come along with my job here at the church. Apparently, unbeknownst to myself, I've developed the idea that being a pastor makes me somebody.

During training, I've also started realizing what an ivory tower we all live in, not only me as a pastor but all of us as islanders. It's easy to take for granted the beauty and spaciousness of our rural island home. Waiting for two or three cars at a stop sign feels like traffic jam here on Vashon, but over in the city, people are just piled on top of people. The vast, sprawling apartment complexes are jammed right next to freeways, around the corner from truck yards, and down the street from warehouses and factories. There's constant noise. We pulled into a gas station and cars were everywhere. People were busy wherever you looked. There was a man blowing leaves off the curb with a leaf blower, and others doing endless jobs of all kinds. We went into a commercial bakery, donning hairnets (including one over my beard) to dig around for our order, and I realized these folks pushing carts all over the factory spend their whole day, minus lunch and possibly smoke breaks, in a massive, concrete, windowless building. The tree and the bench out front were a paradise in that context, whereas I live where the trees outnumber people a hundred to one, my office has windows, and I don't even have to work in my office if I don't want to.

One shop we went into was quite small. There were just two people working there when we walked in—a manager and one employee. Kevin, my trainer, knew them both well and we spent quite a bit of time chatting with both. First, we talked to the employee, a man I'll call Sam. He and Kevin bantered back and forth for a minute and then we went into the office. The manager was slumped over his desk with a stack of checks and an adding machine. "I can't stop, guys. If I stop, the adding machine turns off and I have to do this all over again." He cursed his unreliable bookkeeper, who was nowhere to be seen, and kept punching numbers. Halfway through our conversation the phone rang. Without stopping punching numbers, the manager answered the phone. Kevin and I stood there stupidly for a few minutes and then gestured to him that we were leaving.

By the time we got back to the main part of the shop Sam had finished loading our van. He and Kevin started talking again, and then Sam brought us over to his desk. On top of the computer tower, on top of Sam's desk, were three little matchbox cars. "Look at these," Sam said. "Just picked these up the other day." Kevin looked very interested, but I was confused. As Sam showed us the toy cars and talked all about them, I began to think maybe he was a little weird. Why was he so excited about toy cars? Why did he want us to see them? I didn't understand, but tried to play along. I complimented one of the cars, the one Sam seemed most proud of. "Here, you can have it," he said, putting the car in my hand. "Oh," I said dumbly, "Um, no thanks. That's really nice of you, but you can keep it," I said, putting the car back on his desk.

After we finished talking and went outside, Kevin told me about Sam.

Sam, it turns out, used to be homeless. He's suffered from several addictions and has actually been fired from the very shop we were in twice before. But after his last bout with addiction, Sam went into rehab and got clean. Recovery seems to be sticking this time, and one of the things Sam is now putting his energy into, instead of gambling and beer, is collecting matchbox cars. "He's given me quite a few," said Kevin, "I don't feel like I should take them. He spends his money on them. But I also don't want to seem unappreciative. So now I've got a whole bunch."

What I hadn't understood about Sam's matchbox cars was that they are, in the context of Sam's addiction, a vehicle of redemption. Sam needs to focus on something, to care about something. And collecting toy cars makes him feel good. They give him something to think about and something to do. Giving them away, I imagine, makes him feel even better. I wish I had kept the one he had given me. But I expect that I'll see Sam again.

The fifth fundamental truth of the Assemblies of God reads like this:

> *"Man's only hope of redemption is through the shed blood of Jesus Christ the Son of God. Salvation is received through repentance toward God and faith toward our Lord Jesus Christ. By the washing of regeneration and renewing of the Holy Spirit, being justified by grace through faith, man becomes an heir of God according to the hope of eternal life. The inward evidence of salvation is the direct witness of the Spirit. The outward evidence to all men is a life of righteousness and true holiness."*

SALVATION

In this series, we've already thought about God, the Bible, Jesus, and sin. There is a God who made us and who loves us. The Bible tells us his story. Jesus is the one in whom all of God's plans come together. He is God for us and with us. He is our brother, being fully human. And he is our savior, being fully divine. We've seen that sin is an issue that stems fully from us, not just as individuals but as a group. God is good and has made our lives to be good. We have given in to the temptation to live life without God, and in the process, we've made a mess of our lives and God's world. And now our statement of faith begins telling us how God is fixing that problem.

The biblical word for God's solution to sin is "salvation." The word can mean healing and rescue. In saving us, God rescues us. And in rescuing us, God heals us. And the way God heals us, we are told, is through the death of Jesus Christ on the cross, accessed by us through grace-empowered repentance and faith.

The Bible passage we read this morning is perhaps a familiar one. In it, Jesus is approached by a religious leader at night named Nicodemus. Nicodemus and his fellow religious leaders know Jesus is from God, but they also consider him a bit of a threat. So Nicodemus comes to Jesus at night, hoping nobody will see. He tries to start a conversation with Jesus, but Jesus just starts talking in riddles. Jesus tells Nicodemus he must be "born again." He tells him about being born of water and the Spirit. Human flesh can only create more human flesh, Jesus says. But God's Spirit can give birth to more spirit. Like a blowing wind, God can come in and move everything around. You can't see God, but you can sense him. That's how it is with everyone who is born of the Spirit.

Nicodemus, of course, is confused. But instead of agreeing with Nicodemus that this stuff can be confusing, Jesus instead scolds him for not already knowing all this. The Hebrew Bible is full of references to new life, after all. Moses told God's people to circumcise their hearts, for one thing. That was clearly a metaphor about being changed on the inside. Jeremiah promised a new covenant where God would write his laws on people's hearts and put a new spirit inside them. And Ezekiel promised that God would sprinkle his people with water and give them a new spirit and a new heart. That's what Jesus was talking about, and Nicodemus should have understood it. But that's okay, Jesus then seems to say. Even if Nicodemus can't understand something as earthy as being born again, God will still do what Nicodemus can't. God is going to lift his Son up on a cross, and when people like Nicodemus see it and believe, this new birth Jesus is talking about—prophesied, mysterious, and invisible—will take place, even in people like Nicodemus who haven't, up to this point, understood. God's people will have a new start, and that new start will take place when they turn their eyes toward Jesus on the cross.

You and I need a new start, too, of course. One doesn't live too long without realizing that. Sometimes it feels like we need a new start every day. Like Sam, we all have things holding us down—choices we've made, addictions we can't kick, pains that won't heal. And like Sam with his cars, we need somewhere to look. Looking to ourselves hasn't done us any good. We need something, outside of ourselves, on which to place our hope and our trust. We can't just do the same thing again and again, hoping somehow this time it will be different. We need help from outside. We need what Jesus called the new birth.

I don't know if Sam believes in Jesus. If not, I hope someday he does. But I do know that matchbox cars aren't what's really giving Sam the power to stay clean. God is teaching Sam something about faith. Faith isn't just believing things that are hard to believe. Faith is focusing on something, casting yourself onto it, and letting it make you new. It's what theologian Paul Tillich called having an "ultimate concern." Matchbox cars won't get Sam into heaven, but maybe matchbox cars are something of a start.

One day, if he doesn't already know it, I hope Sam learns that God is the one who gave him those cars. And I hope he comes to find out, if he doesn't already know it, that God gave Sam something else, too. God gave Sam a Savior, Jesus Christ. This Savior entered into a life like the life Sam lives. And this Savior has gone to a cross for Sam's salvation, for yours, and for mine. And if, like with those cars, Sam looks away from his addictions and looks

SALVATION

toward Jesus on the cross, he will find the source of the healing he's begun to taste already in a small but measurable way. He will find himself saved, rescued, and made new. He will find himself born again.

Let's Pray

6.

The Ordinances of the Church (Baptism and Communion)

38 Peter replied, "Repent and be baptized, every one of you, in the name of Jesus Christ for the forgiveness of your sins. And you will receive the gift of the Holy Spirit. **39** The promise is for you and your children and for all who are far off—for all whom the Lord our God will call."

40 With many other words he warned them; and he pleaded with them, "Save yourselves from this corrupt generation." **41** Those who accepted his message were baptized, and about three thousand were added to their number that day.

42 They devoted themselves to the apostles' teaching and to fellowship, to the breaking of bread and to prayer. **43** Everyone was filled with awe at the many wonders and signs performed by the apostles. **44** All the believers were together and had everything in common. **45** They sold property and possessions to give to anyone who had need. **46** Every day they continued to meet together in the temple courts. They broke bread in their homes and ate together with glad and sincere hearts, **47** praising God and enjoying the favor of all the people. And the Lord added to their number daily those who were being saved.

Acts 2:38–47

THE ORDINANCES OF THE CHURCH

IN SOME WAYS, I don't think we really think about our relationships with people until they die.

This might seem a strange thing to say at first. We think about our relationships with the people in our lives all the time. While the people with whom we share life remain alive, our relationships with them remain a work in progress. But should news come to us that someone we know has died, our relationship to them enters a sudden state of completion.

Even for those of us who believe in the immortality of the soul, there is still something very final about death. We can't really picture heaven, beyond what seems like a child's imagination, so until we see them again, or we all stand before God, that person really is gone. Who and how we were to them, and who and how they were to us, can now be weighed and measured in its entirety. It's not always a comforting project (though sometimes it really can be), but it's something we all have to do.

In the past two weeks, I've had two very different experiences with death. First was the performance of a graveside memorial for a person I'd only met a few times. I did not really know her, but I know the family and was asked to lead the service. Everything I wrote and planned to say had to be oriented toward what I knew of the individual through her family. I had to be very careful not to assume too much. I'm sure some of what I said was inaccurate. But the family showed me grace and appreciated what I said. As people shared, during the service, their appreciation and memories of their dearly departed, I did my best to listen vigilantly and compassionately. It was my opportunity to make sure, even as the service itself was taking place, that my tone, words, and expressions were appropriate. The service was entirely for others. Death, for me, in that moment, was an abstraction.

The other recent experience with death was receiving the news that a woman whom I have pastored for over a decade, and known far longer than that, passed away: Helen Jennings.

I've known Helen since I was a grocery cashier in my early 20's. She and her mom, whom Helen was caregiving at the time, would come through the store several times a week. Her mom was

A BASIS OF FELLOWSHIP

a character, as was Helen, and in many ways she gave Helen quite the runaround. I don't remember the name of Helen's mother, but I do remember she was a flirt. On more than one occasion, she would try to pinch the backsides of men as she walked through the store. At least once or twice, I think she succeeded. This, of course, horrified Helen. They'd argue in voices you could hear several aisles away, but it was a sort of playful arguing. Helen also had her wild side, and she clearly found her mother both exasperating and hilarious.

Years later, Helen and her husband Rick became my cheerleaders and loyal critics here at VICC. Rick usually had a problem with something I'd said in my sermon, and Helen would mostly tell me the parts where I got animated were the good parts. Rick and Helen had their ups and downs over the years, as some of us know, until a few years ago when their health declined quickly and dramatically. For a variety of reasons, this led to long nights for me at their house and dozens of hospital visits. It was in the height of COVID in 2020, and Helen considered my presence in the hospital something supernatural because no one else was allowed to visit anyone else in any of the other rooms. Having different needs, Rick and Helen were separated and wound up at different health facilities. Rick's dementia, and further distance away, meant pastoral visits from me were deemed unnecessary, but I made a point of visiting Helen down in Olympia at least once or twice a month. Over the course of time, these visits stretched to once every two months. Then three. Then I didn't visit her for six months or more before heading off to sabbatical at the start of this year, which means I failed to visit her for almost a year in one stretch.

Having returned from my sabbatical this past April, I continued to do a terrible job visiting Helen. She was one of the first people I saw after getting back to work (because she called me once during sabbatical), but then I didn't go down again for a couple of months. A mutual friend reached out to me over the summer and told me Helen's health was further declining, so I made a point of going to see her that very week. I visited her two weeks in a row, but then was out of town again on a family trip. In September, I visited her twice. And I was going to go visit her this past week when I received the call she had died. The finality of her death brought to clear contrast for me how spotty my pastoral care for her had become.

The 6th Fundamental Truth of the Assemblies of God reads like this:

> "The ordinance of baptism by immersion is commanded in the Scriptures. All who repent and believe on Christ as Savior and Lord are to be baptized. Thus they declare to the world that they have died with Christ and that they also have been raised with Him to walk in newness of life. The Lord's Supper, consisting of the elements—bread and the fruit of the vine—is the symbol expressing our sharing the divine nature of our Lord Jesus Christ; a memorial of His suffering and death; and a prophecy of His second coming; and is enjoined on all believers 'till He come!'"

What sticks out to me first in the descriptions of both of these Christian ordinances—baptism and the Lord's Supper—is that they are both symbols of death. The water of baptism, particularly when someone is submerged in it as opposed to having a little bit sprinkled on her head, is a grave. When the believer in Jesus is dunked into the waters of baptism, we are declaring her death. And the Lord's Supper is a symbol of flesh and blood,—broken body and poured-out blood, at that. And we are eating it. From a certain angle, it's a gruesome picture. Little wonder the ancient Romans accused the early Christians of being cannibals. But of course, these symbols are not first of our death, but of Christ's. They are only our death, too, if we identify ourselves with his death, recognize that his death is our death, and enter into the cross-carrying life of following him.

But they are more than symbols of death. We don't simply dunk the believer down into the water and leave her there. We pull her back up. We resurrect her. Or, rather, God does, and we celebrate that in her baptism. She dies, and she rises again, because Christ has died for her and risen again for her, too. And the symbols of Christ's body and blood, the bread and drink of the

A BASIS OF FELLOWSHIP

Christian meal, are also, we are told, a prophecy of Jesus' second coming. Jesus died, but he rose again. And he did not just come once, but he is coming again. The symbols are not of death only, but also of life—life everlasting. That is their comfort and power.

The passage I read at the beginning of the sermon, from Acts 2, is a scene we could call the birth of the church. The Holy Spirit has been poured out on the followers of Jesus (something we will consider next week). Peter has preached the first Christian sermon. The crowd, many of them, are cut to their hearts and ask, "Brothers, what shall we do?" Peter enjoins them to be baptized. And when those who accept Peter's message are baptized, we are told the large crowd is "added to their number"—meaning that, by repentance and water baptism, these new believers are now part of the church.

And the text goes on. The people don't just remain a number. They become a community, a people. They spend their lives together and share their goods. They worship together and pray together. They go to temple together and meet in each other's homes. And, we are told, they break bread together, too.

This breaking bread, of course, refers to eating together. But commentators are also sure it means they celebrated communion. In the ancient church, the communion meal took place within a larger meal the Christians called *agape*, or "love." The meal was a celebration of their union with Christ, but also a celebration of their union with each other. As the apostle Paul will later tell the Corinthians, "Because there is one loaf, we, who are many, are one body, for we all share the one loaf" (1 Corinthians 10:17). And so, by repentance and faith, and celebration of baptism and the Lord's Supper, these new believers became a part of each other's lives. Their lives, intertwined with Christ, were intertwined with each other's as well.

If I have any regrets about my relationship with Helen, it's that, as her pastor, I had started to treat visiting her like a job. Don't get me wrong. We loved each other and I was always glad to go visit. But news of her death brought an immediate pang of regret. I was always so busy, and she was always so alone. And now, with her passing, I will always be the person who said, "I'll see you next week" and then didn't make it down for a month. I'll always be the person to whom Helen said, "It's okay, honey, I know you're busy," every time I made an excuse. I will always, in this life, be the person who allowed pastoring her to become a task. Not when I was with her, per se, but when I was looking where to fit visiting her into my calendar.

But being Helen's pastor wasn't a task, just as being your pastor isn't really a job. As baptized believers in Jesus Christ, you and I—Helen and I—are one. We are *body*. And our eating together every Sunday, and our celebrating water baptism when a person declares her faith, is a recognition that our unity is something more than a social, professional, or functional choice. You and I are bound to each other. We are buried together, risen together, and waiting together for God. It's not a reality we live out very well much of the time, but it's a reality that is truer than the things we do (sometimes every day) that seem to contradict it.

If I have learned anything from these last two weeks, it's that death is an inevitability for us all, and that the apparent finality of death leaves every relationship that is interrupted by death feeling both final and incomplete. But the meal we are about to eat is a reminder that death is still less real than life, and that death is not God's final word.

Let's Pray

7.

The Baptism in the Holy Spirit

1:1 *In my former book, Theophilus, I wrote about all that Jesus began to do and to teach* **2** *until the day he was taken up to heaven, after giving instructions through the Holy Spirit to the apostles he had chosen.* **3** *After his suffering, he presented himself to them and gave many convincing proofs that he was alive. He appeared to them over a period of forty days and spoke about the kingdom of God.* **4** *On one occasion, while he was eating with them, he gave them this command: "Do not leave Jerusalem, but wait for the gift my Father promised, which you have heard me speak about.* **5** *For John baptized with water, but in a few days you will be baptized with the Holy Spirit."*

6 *Then they gathered around him and asked him, "Lord, are you at this time going to restore the kingdom to Israel?"*

7 *He said to them: "It is not for you to know the times or dates the Father has set by his own authority.* **8** *But you will receive power when the Holy Spirit comes on you; and you will be my witnesses in Jerusalem, and in all Judea and Samaria, and to the ends of the earth."*

9 *After he said this, he was taken up before their very eyes, and a cloud hid him from their sight.*

10 *They were looking intently up into the sky as he was going, when suddenly two men dressed in white stood beside them.* **11** *"Men of Galilee," they said, "why do you stand here looking into the sky? This same Jesus, who has been taken from you into heaven, will come back in the same way you have seen him go into heaven."*

Acts 1:1–11

THEY SAY HUMILITY IS one virtue which, to the extent you think you have it, you probably don't.

I'm a few weeks into my new ultra-part-time driving job at the grocery store and am now doing the drives on my own. This past Wednesday, I did my regular route, which starts in the morning in Seattle and ends in the afternoon in Tacoma. The last stop is at our sister store, where I pick up various supplies and smaller orders that would be too expensive to have delivered straight to Vashon. My routine when I get to the Tacoma store is to make a counter-clockwise circle through the building, starting in the floral department and ending in the deli. I check the walk-in fridge behind produce, then the walk-in freezer in the middle back, then the dairy fridge to the left, then the back room by the delivery dock, finally the deli, and then I'm done. Once everything is loaded up in the van, I head to the ferry.

This past week, as I was doing my rounds, the director of the Tacoma store walked up to me and said, "Did you check the dairy fridge?"

"Yeah," I said, "there wasn't anything there."

"Yeah, there is," he said, and walked away. A few minutes later, he came up to me with a shopping cart containing a box and a large bag. "You forgot these last week, too. Clay [the owner] had to take them himself the next day and discount them because of the date."

"Oh," I said, momentarily irritated by his tone. "They weren't where I was told to look. Sorry about that."

"They'll always be in this cart," said the manager, walking away.

A BASIS OF FELLOWSHIP

As I finished loading things in the van, I turned this exchange over and over in my head. Who did this guy think he was? Who was *he* to talk to *me* like that? Doesn't he know I'm a minister? Doesn't he know my wife is a manager at the *larger* store? I'm not doing this job because I need to. I'm doing it meet a few financial goals. I don't need him. He needs me. And who is he, anyway? Just some dumb grocery store manager.

Of course, I'd like to say these weren't the sort of thoughts I was having, but they were. Some of my defensiveness, of course, was from embarrassment. And some of it was simple wounded pride. But some of it, to be honest, was that I'd lost the habit of being spoken to like a servant (or, as we like to call them nowadays, an employee). It's been a decade-and-a-half since my last retail job, and I'd honestly forgotten what it was like being the peon. In ministry, people tell you you're wrong all the time. And often you are. But "Hey pastor, I disagree with that decision you made," is worlds away from, "Hey idiot, you forgot the shopping cart full of pizza dough."

As I drove to the ferry and thought about the exchange, I realized: Who was *he* to walk to *me* like that? He was the boss. And who was *I*? I was the driver who forgot part of his load.

The seventh fundamental truth of the Assemblies of God reads like this,

> *"All believers are entitled to and should ardently expect and earnestly seek the promise of the Father, the baptism in the Holy Spirit and fire, according to the command of our Lord Jesus Christ. This was the normal experience of all in the early Christian church. With it comes the enduement of power for life and service,* [and] *the bestowment of the gifts and their uses in the work of ministry. This experience is distinct from and subsequent to the experience of the new birth. With the baptism in the Holy Spirit come such experiences as an overflowing fullness of the Spirit, a deepened reverence for God, an intensified consecration to God and dedication to His work, and a more active love for Christ, for His Word, and for the lost."*

THE BAPTISM IN THE HOLY SPIRIT

This experience of being baptized in the Holy Spirit is central to what it means to be a Pentecostal Christian. The term is a metaphor, borrowed from the experience of water baptism, and it points to the experience of being submerged or washed in the presence of God.

In our passage today, we see the risen Jesus promising this experience to his disciples. Jesus has gone to the cross and risen again. He's spent forty days teaching his disciples about the kingdom of God. They are anxious to see it fulfilled. "Will you at this time restore the kingdom to Israel?" they ask. "Not yet," Jesus replies, "that's an event reserved for the future. But for now, the world needs to hear about me. And you are the ones who are going to tell them. But not yet. The Father and I need to do one more thing: we need to give you the power of the Spirit."

It's a valid debate whether Jesus is promising the disciples they are about to be born again, or whether he is promising them a distinct charismatic experience. If we know our Bibles, we know what will happen soon. The disciples will be praying. The room will be shaken. The Holy Spirit will enter. We'll look at that episode next week. But what will their experience *be* exactly? Will it be a particularly dramatic example of being born again? Or will their experience be something other than, or more than, the new birth? In what sense(s) will it, as Jesus promises, be a supernatural empowerment from heaven?

To be honest, I think it will be all of the above, and maybe more. We know that Jesus has already told the disciples they are "clean" because of the word he has spoken to them (John 15:3). After his resurrection, according to John 20:22, Jesus physically enacted giving his disciples the Spirit by breathing on them and telling them, "Receive the Holy Spirit." In Paul's letters, we get the sense there is no such thing as believing in Jesus without also receiving the Spirit. "If anyone does not have the Spirit of Christ, they do not belong to Christ" (Romans 8:9b)—a statement that simply can't be interpreted to mean, "If anyone doesn't speak in tongues they aren't going to heaven."

To believe in Jesus is to be made new by the Spirit—full stop. And sometimes, that's a very quiet and invisible event. Just ask any kid who grew up in church: "When did you become a Christian?" More often than not, they'll stare back at you blankly and say something like, "I've always been a Christian." And it's probably not too wise not to believe them. There's no value in sowing doubt in their heart. If they believe in Jesus, and trust him for salvation, they are born of the Spirit. It's as simple as that.

But there's also the experience of being *baptized* in God's Spirit. Dunked, if you will. Submerged. It's an encounter with God that builds faith. *"Wow! God is real!"* And the faith that is born of such an encounter is, I believe, the power Jesus is talking about. It's not that some Christians have more juice in them than others, or that the body of Christ contains first and second class believers. It's that all Christians could stand to trust God a bit more. And that trust has got to come from somewhere. For many, and potentially (I believe) for all, it comes from a baptism into the heavenly presence of God.

Jesus promised his disciples a power that would make them witnesses to the furthest parts of the world. We need that power, too, because one of those "furthest parts" is right here: Vashon Island. And when I think about the pride with which I responded to that manager this past week, I think the power I need from God is the power to *serve*. Because isn't that what the mission of the church really is? Don't we go into the world with the good news of Jesus as an act of service to God? And don't we live in Christian community for the sake of serving each other? And isn't life in the world, for a Christian at least, a life of serving our neighbors in love? It's easy and sentimental to talk about this sort of stuff in church. It's much harder when Monday rolls back around. And that's why we need the power of God.

You and I, as Christian believers, live in the "time-between-times," the space between Jesus' ascension into heaven and his return for his church. God's plan between those two events is to infiltrate the world with a Spirit-baptized and powerful, yet humble and servant-hearted, church. The mission of God doesn't happen without service, and the Spirit's power is given for mission.

Let's Pray

8.

Speaking in Tongues

2:1 When the day of Pentecost came, they were all together in one place. **2** Suddenly a sound like the blowing of a violent wind came from heaven and filled the whole house where they were sitting. **3** They saw what seemed to be tongues of fire that separated and came to rest on each of them. **4** All of them were filled with the Holy Spirit and began to speak in other tongues as the Spirit enabled them.

5 Now there were staying in Jerusalem God-fearing Jews from every nation under heaven. **6** When they heard this sound, a crowd came together in bewilderment, because each one heard their own language being spoken. **7** Utterly amazed, they asked: "Aren't all these who are speaking Galileans? **8** Then how is it that each of us hears them in our native language? **9** Parthians, Medes and Elamites; residents of Mesopotamia, Judea and Cappadocia, Pontus and Asia, **10** Phrygia and Pamphylia, Egypt and the parts of Libya near Cyrene; visitors from Rome **11** (both Jews and converts to Judaism); Cretans and Arabs—we hear them declaring the wonders of God in our own tongues!" **12** Amazed and perplexed, they asked one another, "What does this mean?"

13 Some, however, made fun of them and said, "They have had too much wine."

Acts 2:1–13

SPEAKING IN TONGUES

I USED TO HAVE a quote on my wall from the late, great Jerry Garcia, lead singer for the Grateful Dead. It said something along the lines of, "Our band is like black licorice. People who like us *really* like us. People who hate us *really* hate us." I think something similar can be said about speaking in tongues.

Several years ago, an Episcopal woman I knew approached me about the topic of speaking in tongues. She wasn't interested in the experience for herself, but she did want to know what I thought of it. In her younger years, during the charismatic renewal of the 1970s, some people she knew had tried to get her to speak in tongues. The whole experience was strange and uncomfortable, and it alienated her from her friends. Now, years later, she saw that I had written a social media post on the topic and became curious. Apparently, she considered me somewhat less insane than her charismatic friends of decades ago, and the fact that I seemed to have a not-entirely-negative view of the experience sparked her interest. What did I think of speaking in tongues?

I asked if she had ever found herself in a situation where she didn't know what to say. Maybe something was so wonderful she was speechless, or maybe something was so terrible she couldn't bring herself to say anything. She acknowledged that she had. I asked if she had ever had that sort of experience in her prayer life. Had she ever been so sad that all she could do was sit before God and sigh? Had she ever been in a place in her life where her tears or her laughter amounted to a prayer, perhaps the only prayer she could produce in that moment? She had. I told her about Paul's words in Romans chapter 8 about creation groaning as it awaits redemption, and about how we groan, too, as we long for resurrection. Then I pointed out that Paul says God's Spirit also groans, through us, when we no longer know how to pray—the "wordless groans" of the Spirit joining with our own groans as we sit before God, unsure what to say anymore. These inarticulate prayers rise to the Father, who knows all things, carried from us to God by God's Spirit.

A BASIS OF FELLOWSHIP

"Sitting before God and laughing, sighing, crying, or groaning because you simply don't know what to say anymore, is not too far from what I know of speaking in tongues," I told her.

"Well," she replied, "I've never spoken in some magical language before, but I've certainly prayed like that many times."

The eighth fundamental truth of the Assemblies of God is titled, "The Initial Physical Evidence of the Baptism in the Holy Spirit," and it reads like this:

> "The baptism of believers in the Holy Spirit is witnessed by the initial physical sign of speaking with other tongues as the Spirit of God gives them utterance. The speaking in tongues in this instance is the same in essence as the gift of tongues, but different in purpose and use."

This statement is derived from the experience of the disciples on the first Christian Pentecost in Acts chapter 2 (which we just read) and is written with an eye toward answering the question, "How do I know if I've been baptized in the Holy Spirit?"

In this passage, the promise Jesus gave his disciples in Acts chapter one—that they would soon receive the Spirit's power—is fulfilled. The disciples are waiting in Jerusalem, as commanded, when the day of Pentecost arrives. Pentecost is the Greek name for the Jewish Feast of Weeks, a spring harvest festival celebrating the first crop of wheat. And it's on this day, a day celebrating harvest, that the promise of the Father arrives. The place where the disciples are gathered is suddenly shaken, and the sound of wind fills their ears. Flames of fire, like what Moses saw at the burning bush, appear above the disciples' heads. The Spirit of God fills each one of their hearts, and they begin praying in languages they've never learned. The Holy Spirit has come.

The disciples are almost certainly gathered in some part of the Temple complex when this happens. We can guess this because the commotion quickly draws a crowd. What the crowd sees and hears confuses them immensely. Most of them are pilgrims from other parts of the Roman Empire in town for the feast. They are all Jews or converts to Judaism, and they all presumably speak either Aramaic or Greek—the common language of the Near East and the common language of the Empire, respectively. But they also have their own languages from wherever they're from. As they gather to see what all the noise is about, they stumble upon a throng of Galileans from up north singing and praising God—not in Hebrew, Aramaic, or Greek, but in the native languages of the pilgrim crowd.

Of course, not everyone is impressed. While one person says, "They're speaking my language!" and another says, "I swear, they're speaking *my* language!" still others in the crowd hear nothing but gibberish. These latter just scoff, "Oh it's nothing but a bunch of drunks from up north!" A miracle of some kind has definitely taken place, but it's not a miracle to all. Just like in the earthly life of Jesus, where some encountered the Son of God while others encountered a heretic and a threat, so in the outpouring of the Holy Spirit, some hear the wonderful works of God being proclaimed while others hear nothing but nonsense. Grace seems to be at work in both speaker and hearer at the outpouring of the Spirit on that first Christian Pentecost, but for those who were not open to a new thing from God, they heard and saw nothing but madness.

It's a very controversial claim for Pentecostals to make, that there is a second work of grace called the baptism in the Holy Spirit and that it is evidenced by speaking in tongues. Not every Christian would agree that there are further fillings of the Spirit beyond one's conversion, and even for those who do, not all would agree that you always (or even ever) speak in tongues. And even the most dogged classical Pentecostal will admit that the Spirit is alive and well in all who believe in Jesus, and that spiritual gifts are also at work in the lives of those who don't speak in tongues. Some will even admit that, for one reason or another, even those who are *filled* with the Spirit will not always speak in tongues. Nevertheless, a link remains between the gift and the experience, and I think this has to be explored.

My Episcopal friend at the beginning of the sermon was among those who find speaking in tongues just plain weird. Sometimes when people pray in tongues, they do seem to be praying in a real language, however unidentifiable that language might be.

But sometimes it just sounds like their insides are coming out. In Paul's first letter to the Corinthians, he warns his readers to keep praying in tongues to a mostly private affair—because if unbelievers or Christians who don't know much about spiritual gifts walk into your service, they're going to think you're nuts! Paul loves praying privately in tongues, but he thinks church is mostly about words people can understand. He doesn't seem entirely concerned that people's prayer languages be in actually identifiable human dialects, and there's even evidence in the text he doesn't always think they are. For tongues to mean anything to anyone but the speaker and God, a gift of speaking and a gift of hearing have to be at play—a sensitivity to the Spirit in both parties, a heart for God and a heart for those gathered around. At Pentecost, it seemed to be a miracle of hearing. In the gathered church, it's the gift of interpretation.

When Paul talks about praying in tongues, he says, "My spirit prays, but my mind is unfruitful" (1 Corinthians 14:14). Praying in the Spirit is about coming to the end of oneself, like what I said to my Episcopalian friend about running out of words. And this is where I think the link between speaking in tongues and being baptized in the Holy Spirit come together: *Speaking in tongues is embarrassing.* Some people take pride in it, of course, but most people who do it feel kind of stupid until they've done it for a while—and many, like me, would rather hit themselves with a hammer than stand up in front of a bunch of people and do it out loud! It's something that arises from a heart's encounter with God. It's very intimate and very awkward and very easy to doubt. I do think it's a language, but it's a language that finds its source and purpose in the Spirit. I'm not really worried that it's not Swahili or French. Prayer in the Spirit can be joyful or heartbroken, desperate or excited. Whatever one's experience, what prayer in the Spirit always has in common is the coming to the end of oneself in the best possible way. And *that*, I believe, is the link between praying in tongues and being filled with God's Spirit.

God's Spirit indwells every person who calls on Jesus' name, and the Spirit gives gifts to each and every one of us. Being *less* full of ourselves is the key to being *more* full of God, whether we speak in tongues or we don't. When we come to the end of ourselves, and even the end of our ability to pray, we come to a point of being uniquely enabled to be filled with the fullness of God. This applies to our doctrine, our morality, our churches, our families, our lives, and even the tongues in our mouths. The person who runs out of self is in a good place to get filled with God. The same applies to the person who runs out of words.

Let's Pray

9.

Sanctification (Holiness)

5:1 *Follow God's example, therefore, as dearly loved children* 2 *and walk in the way of love, just as Christ loved us and gave himself up for us as a fragrant offering and sacrifice to God.*

3 *But among you there must not be even a hint of sexual immorality, or of any kind of impurity, or of greed, because these are improper for God's holy people.* 4 *Nor should there be obscenity, foolish talk or coarse joking, which are out of place, but rather thanksgiving.* 5 *For of this you can be sure: No immoral, impure or greedy person—such a person is an idolater—has any inheritance in the kingdom of Christ and of God.* 6 *Let no one deceive you with empty words, for because of such things God's wrath comes on those who are disobedient.* 7 *Therefore do not be partners with them.*

8 *For you were once darkness, but now you are light in the Lord. Live as children of light* 9 *(for the fruit of the light consists in all goodness, righteousness and truth)* 10 *and find out what pleases the Lord.* 11 *Have nothing to do with the fruitless deeds of darkness, but rather expose them.* 12 *It is shameful even to mention what the disobedient do in secret.* 13 *But everything exposed by the light becomes visible—and everything that is illuminated becomes a light.* 14 *This is why it is said:*

SANCTIFICATION (HOLINESS)

*"Wake up, sleeper,
rise from the dead,
and Christ will shine on you."*

Ephesians 5:1–14

I ONCE HEARD A preacher say that every "yes" is also a "no." Every decision to do something is also a decision not to do something else. Every decision to go somewhere is also a decision not to go somewhere else. The preacher was speaking in the context of a wedding, and he was telling the young couple what their vows really meant. To say "I do" to one another was to say "I don't" to anyone else.

The ninth fundamental truth of the Assemblies of God is on the doctrine of sanctification and it reads, in part, like this:

> *"Sanctification is an act of separation from that which is evil, and of dedication unto God. [The] Scriptures teach a life of 'holiness without which no man shall see the Lord'. By the power of the Holy Spirit we are able to obey the command: 'Be ye holy, for I am holy'."*

This is the kind of language that tends to lose us today. Words like "sanctification" and "holiness" either don't mean anything to us at all, or they don't mean anything good. "Sanctification" sounds like "sanctimonious," and "holy" sounds like "holier than thou." Ours is a day in which the church has been exposed as a flawed institution, no matter what the tradition, and those Christians who have tried to act as though they were above the petty sins of the world have been exposed as no better than anyone else—and sometimes as something far worse. Holiness has fallen on hard times, not only as a concept but also as a reality.

When I was on sabbatical earlier this year, one of the books I read was a little tract written by a preacher named John Wesley almost 300 years ago. The book was called *A Plain Account of Christian Perfection* and it was written as an answer to Wesley's critics. John Wesley and some of his companions had become the central figures of a controversy about whether Christians could truly become sinless in this life. Many people believed the idea was preposterous, but Wesley believed it could happen. In fact, he claimed to have seen it happen many times. Though in private correspondence he confessed to never attaining perfection himself, in his little book Wesley gave several accounts of people he believed had experienced it. Understandably, Wesley's critics thought he was a fanatic. And I'll admit his ideas aren't above criticism. But as I read his little book and got a better sense of what Wesley was saying, he helped me gain a new understanding of what sanctification really means.

John Wesley believed that true holiness, or what he called "Christian perfection," was a matter of the heart more than a matter of the outward life. It had a direct effect on the outward life, of course, but what Wesley called "perfection" had to do with a person's *affections* or his loves. Jesus taught his disciples that all God's commands could be summed up in love: love for God and love for people. And Jesus had also commanded his disciples, "Be ye perfect, as your Farther in heaven is perfect." If Jesus could command us to love God and each other, and to be "perfect" (or complete, or mature) in our love the same way God is, then it stood to reason this was something God could bring about. Wesley wasn't I to our sinfulness, of course. He didn't think we could do this all on our own. We needed forgiveness and salvation, first of all. We needed to be born again. And having been forgiven, we needed to *desire* holiness before we could ever receive it. But as our salvation did its work in our hearts, and a hunger and thirst for righteousness grew in our souls, Wesley believed we could start pursuing God to make us completely holy. And so he believed that what God commanded of us God could also provide. If we asked God to make us holy, God in his mercy just might do it.

Interestingly, when Wesley talked about those whom he believed had attained Christian perfection, he still wrote of them as people who needed forgiveness. They still lived in the weakness of human flesh, and they still stumbled and fell short in many ways. But it was their *loves* that had changed, and that's what Wesley called their Christian perfection. Their bitterness was gone. The

SANCTIFICATION (HOLINESS)

assurance of God's goodness was there. A deep and abiding peace had appeared in their hearts. What Wesley meant by "Christian perfection" was the spiritual gift of being perfected in love, baptized (if you will) with God's love. Being holy, for Wesley, meant being a person who *loved*. And for me, that was a very helpful insight.

In our passage this morning, the apostle Paul is giving his Ephesian readers the "herefore" of all the previous theology he has given them in this letter. God has saved you by his grace, Paul said in chapter 2, "therefore. . ." You have been lifted from death and given new life through Jesus, Paul has said, "therefore. . ." You Gentile Christians, to whom the promises of the Old Testament were largely not written, are now included in the covenant community with all of its promises because of Jesus, "therefore. . ." As the old adage goes, whenever you see the word "therefore," you go back and see what it's there for. And in chapters 4 through 6 of Ephesians, Paul is applying the logic of his gospel teaching from chapters 1 through 3 to the daily realities of Christian life.

Not unlike his student of many centuries later, John Wesley, the apostle Paul also grounds Christian life and obedience in love. "Follow God's example," Paul says. Or, as the English Standard Version has it, "Be imitators of God." And how are we to imitate God? By acting like Jesus. Jesus went to the cross for us when we were his enemies. He chose life with us instead of life without us. He forgave, he redeemed, and he saved. In his earthly life, he healed the sick, he raised the dead, and he welcomed the outcast. He cared for the poor and he shared what he had with the needy. He lived his life in the confidence that he was loved by his heavenly Father, and that his Father's love should extend through him and beyond him to the world. "Be like that," Paul says. "Act like Jesus. Be an imitator of God."

Being an imitator of God is saying yes to salvation, yes to grace, and yes to love. But as we go on in our passage, we learn that being an imitator of God means saying "no" to things as well. Like the couple at the wedding whom the preacher told that saying "I do" to each other meant saying "I don't" to anyone else, we learn that in following Jesus we say "yes" to love, so we also say "no" to greed. We say "yes" to sexual faithfulness, so we say "no" sexual sin. We say "yes" to gratitude and encouragement, so we therefore say "no" to cruel joking that tears people down instead of building them up. We say yes, and in saying yes, we also say no.

Life with God is a beautiful journey. It's a journey of saying "yes" to God and being perfected, in this life and the next, by his grace. But the journey with God is also a journey of saying "no": no to sin and no to hate. No to selfishness, no to laziness, and no to lust. And we don't say no *so that* God will love us or *so that* God will save us, but rather *because* God has loved us and *because* God has saved us. The wrath of God is real, but for us who believe, it's been dealt with at the cross.

"For you were once darkness, but now you are light in the Lord. *Live* as children of light."

Let's Pray

10.

The Church

1:1 *Paul, called to be an apostle of Christ Jesus by the will of God, and our brother Sosthenes,*

2 To the church of God in Corinth, to those sanctified in Christ Jesus and called to be his holy people, together with all those everywhere who call on the name of our Lord Jesus Christ—their Lord and ours:

3 Grace and peace to you from God our Father and the Lord Jesus Christ.

1 Corinthians 1:1–3

ONE OF THE MORE intimidating things about being a parent is realizing your child is going to look at you, through the various stages of her life, in about the same way you looked at your parents when you were going through those same stages. This isn't universally true, of course. We didn't all grow up with our parents, and even those of us who did didn't always have the healthiest ones. But assuming our parents were present and made a reasonable effort, and that we are present and are making a reasonable effort ourselves (if we're parents), there's a certain mirror experience to it all.

Parents begin their journey being everything to their children: provider, protector, guide, teacher, and friend. But as the

A BASIS OF FELLOWSHIP

child grows and gets older, the magic that is "mommy" and "daddy" begins to fade. Mom and dad are still good, but they stop being perfect. As adolescence progresses, mom and dad even begin to seem kind of stupid at times. They don't know what any slang means. Their taste in music is wretched. They become more than a little critical of some of our favorite friends. And clearly, they have no idea what it's like being a kid!

As we enter adulthood, somewhere between ages twenty and twenty-five, our parents start to know what they're talking about again—to some degree, at least. And sometime before we reach thirty, our parents (usually) stop being idiots. But then it's not long before we start providing for our parents instead of the other way around. Assuming tragedy doesn't befall us, this process will continue and grow all the way to our parents' death, at which point we (now adults for some years) will have something like a "complete view" of our parents: not perfect, but also far from the fools we once thought they were; flawed, but also complex; a mixture of good and bad; people who tried their best, who passed on lessons to us, who lived through the challenge of human existence; people who, in some way, were a lesson just by being themselves.

When I think of the church, it makes me think of this parent-child relationship. Not everyone who has grown up in church, or has passed through the church, considers it a good experience, of course. Just as there are broken families, so there are broken churches and broken Christians. But for those of us who never leave, who enter as converts, or who eventually return, our relationship with the church is not unlike that childhood journey. First the church knows everything, then the church knows nothing. At some point, we grow up and see that, though the church isn't perfect, she is still good. As we get older, we realize we are as responsible for the church as the church is for us, so we care for the church as the church has cared for us. And after a long life of involvement, we develop perspective on the church. We look on all her flaws and all her triumphs. We look on her with a mixture of gratitude and sadness, hope and humor, regret and deep love. Church, the communion of saints, is our mother just as God is our

Father. She's not perfect, but she is the one through whom God our Father has chosen to give us life through the gospel. She is us and we are her. The church has raised us up, and now we ourselves are the church.

The tenth fundamental truth of the Assemblies of God, on the doctrine of the church, reads in part:

> "The church is the body of Christ, the habitation of God through the Spirit, with divine appointments for the fulfillment of her Great Commission. Each believer, born of the Spirit, is an integral part of the general assembly and church of the first-born, which are written in heaven."

Our passage this morning, 1 Corinthians 1:1–3, also summarizes for us what the church is, almost without meaning to. It's Paul's version of the traditional Greco-Roman greeting for a letter. "From so-and-so, To so-and-so: Greetings." Paul changes the Greek word for greeting, *charein*, to the Greek word for grace, *charis*, and adds the Jewish greeting, "peace."

The church Paul writes to, in the ancient Greek city of Corinth, is a handful. If you know the letter, and its companion 2 Corinthians, you know this is a church with a lot of problems. It's a very gifted church. People are very open to the work of the Spirit. But it's also a prideful church and a divided church. The congregation has managed to chop itself up into little cliques. Some of the groups define themselves by their favorite theologian. Others define themselves by their favorite spiritual gift. It seems the members who speak in tongues have a particularly high view of themselves. Sexual sin seems common in the church. Paul literally has to tell them to stop going to prostitutes. Also, a man of some standing in the congregation is having an affair with his mother-in-law and Paul needs to tell the Corinthians that's actually a bad thing. As far as the city of Corinth is concerned, this is a congregation of nobodies. But as far as *they* are all concerned, they are quite the important little group. It's to this headache of a congregation the apostle Paul sends this greeting. And it's the fact that Paul could give such a greeting to such a congregation that tells us so much about church.

A BASIS OF FELLOWSHIP

Paul calls the congregation in Corinth "sanctified." In last week's sermon, we talked about being sanctified, or holy, but I never bothered defining the word. Our focus last week was on what being holy looks like in life: saying yes to Jesus and no to our sin. But the word "sanctified" actually has a definition. Being sanctified means being set apart. A holy person, a holy thing, or a holy place is something that's set apart. The holy man of a village is a very special person. A holy thing, such as a candle or a dish, is something you only use for special purposes, like in a religious ritual. And a holy place is a place you treat with respect, speaking in hushed tones when you're there and perhaps removing your shoes. So being "holy," in the Christian sense, means setting yourself and your life apart to honor Jesus. Like we said last week, it's saying "yes" to Jesus and "no" to sin.

But clearly, when Paul calls this congregation of sinners in Corinth "sanctified," he's not saying they live exemplary lives. What he says, in fact, is that they are sanctified "in Christ Jesus," and that's the key to our understanding of church. The believers living in Corinth are a people that God has set aside. He has attached them to Jesus through the gospel and faith and has set them apart for his own special use. They are the saints of God in the land—bunch of sinners that they are. They are the ones who know Jesus and can talk about him. They are the holy ones of God in the sinful city of Corinth.

This sanctification, of course, has its implications. Not only has God set the Corinthians apart, but they are supposed to set themselves apart, too. God has made them holy and special in Jesus, and their calling is to learn to be what God made. The fact that they are failing to live like saints doesn't change the fact that they are.

As an expression of the people of God here on Vashon, we in this congregation are a holy people of God, too. By our faltering and faulty faith in God's Son, you and I have been made into a special creation of God. Vashon Island Community Church, together with every congregation on this island, are the saints of God in the land. But that doesn't mean we're the "good people" and our neighbors are the "bad." Rather, like Jesus told his original disciples in the Sermon on the Mount, being God's saints means being salt and light in the world. We are the salt Jesus has sprinkled on Vashon. We are the lamp God has lit and put on a high shelf. We are the people God has put here so we can be a witness to the wonderful goodness of God. Like the Corinthians, you and I are not always the best at being what we are. But we are, nevertheless, salt and light, the saints of God in the land.

When people came across Jesus during his earthly life, some encountered God while others met a dangerous heretic. When the Spirit was poured out on Pentecost, some of the crowd heard the wonderful works of God being proclaimed in their native tongues while others heard nothing but nonsense. And when some folks come across that people called "church" today, many see nothing but a mess. Some of this is because of the hiddenness of God, and some is because of our failure to live up to our calling. But a mess is not all that we are. Despite appearances, church is the place where God does his best work. Like the congregation in Corinth, we, too, are a community of sinners. But like them, too, we are also the saints of God in the land. We are salt and light, the community of the redeemed.

Let's Pray

11.

The Ministry

CHRIST THE KING SUNDAY

1 *Then Jesus said to the crowds and to his disciples:* **2** *"The teachers of the law and the Pharisees sit in Moses' seat.* **3** *So you must be careful to do everything they tell you. But do not do what they do, for they do not practice what they preach.* **4** *They tie up heavy, cumbersome loads and put them on other people's shoulders, but they themselves are not willing to lift a finger to move them.*

5 *"Everything they do is done for people to see: They make their phylacteries wide and the tassels on their garments long;* **6** *they love the place of honor at banquets and the most important seats in the synagogues;* **7** *they love to be greeted with respect in the marketplaces and to be called 'Rabbi' by others.*

8 *"But you are not to be called 'Rabbi,' for you have one Teacher, and you are all brothers.* **9** *And do not call anyone on earth 'father,' for you have one Father, and he is in heaven.* **10** *Nor are you to be called instructors, for you have one Instructor, the Messiah.* **11** *The greatest among you will be your servant.* **12** *For those who exalt themselves* *will be humbled, and those who humble themselves will be exalted."*

Matthew 23:1–12

ONE OF THE MORE controversial beliefs in the Assemblies of God, and one that doesn't get explicit mention in our statement of faith, is our belief that both women and men can serve at all levels of church government. Among more theologically liberal churches, this wouldn't be a controversial position at all. But among evangelical traditions, it often still is. And among the church viewed globally and historically (especially if we include Catholic and Orthodox traditions), ours is definitely a minority position.

But while this morning is not the time to walk through all the various biblical issues in that debate—Jesus choosing twelve men to found the church, Paul's prohibitions in 1 Corinthians and 1 Timothy, the prominent role of women in many of Paul's churches, Priscilla taking part in correcting Apollos' doctrine in the book of Acts, the role Phoebe played in delivering Paul's letter to the Romans, and so on—one area of focus that often takes center stage, but one that really shouldn't if we took our New Testaments more seriously, is the debate over who gets to share in, or have access to, *power* in the life of the church.

When Andrew and Jennifer were worshipping with us, Jennifer once asked me about the issue of women in ministry. She had heard the Assemblies of God took what's called an "egalitarian" position on the issue, meaning we believe both men *and* women can lead in the church. Jennifer's background was in the Reformed church, and Andrew's was in conservative Lutheranism, both of which take the more traditional position that only men can serve in church office. But in the denomination Andrew is currently serving, the issue is a bit more open. Some churches believe women can be pastors and some don't.

Andrew's last parish had been next door to a seminary that served students from both the United States and overseas, and Jennifer had been particularly interested in the female students. Because of her own beliefs and church background, Jennifer was skeptical these women should have been training for the pastoral ministry at all, but she also noted a marked difference between two groups of female students. The American students, Jennifer felt, seemed particularly interested in standing up for their "right" to preach. Their focus often struck Jennifer as being, in many ways, about *power*. But the international students (I particularly remember her mentioning some students from Africa) never spoke, as far as Jennifer could remember, about fighting for their rights or standing up to the men. There was a humility in them she didn't always feel like she noticed in their American classmates—even though these women, too, were training to lead churches. In short, the international students didn't strike Jennifer as being in seminary for the sake of *power*.

The eleventh fundamental truth of the Assemblies of God is on the ministry, and it reads like this:

> "A *divinely called and scripturally ordained ministry has been provided by our Lord for the fourfold purpose of leading the church in:* [the] *evangelization of the world,* [the] *worship of God,* [the] *building* [of] *a body of saints being perfected in the image of* [God's] *Son,* [and for] *meeting human need with ministries of love and compassion.*"

In our passage this morning, Jesus is speaking to the crowds and to his disciples about the religious leaders of his day. And everything Jesus has to say about these religious leaders is a warning.

The teachers of the law and the Pharisees—the two parties Jesus mentions—were two different groups of people, even though they are often mentioned together in the Gospels. The teachers of the law had a more official role. They were not priests, but their job was to be experts in the law of Moses. They existed to make sure people honored the Scriptures and followed its mandates. They were the experts in morals, ceremonies, and all other aspects of religion and public life. The Pharisees, on the other hand, were a popular but self-appointed group. They believed the biggest need God's people had was for holiness, and their solution was to teach even non-ordained people to live by all the rules the law of God put on priests. Both groups were very concerned about God, the

Bible, and holy living. But Jesus warns the crowd, and his disciples, against them both.

The first criticism Jesus has for the religious leaders is that they don't practice what they preach. They say one thing and do something else. Tying (or binding) heavy burdens on people refers to the religious leaders' tendency to multiply taboos for people, increasing the number of ways a person might fear they don't please God. But having placed such emotional burdens on people, these religious leaders seem neither to care about the anxiety they produce in others nor to live under such anxiety themselves. While convincing others that God may be mad at them, they walk around confident they themselves please God.

The religious leaders also, according to Jesus, make a show of their piety, and expect to be treated with great respect wherever they go. Titles are very important to them, and religion—for them—is a gateway to power.

Jesus, on the other hand, says his people are to be siblings. Relying, as he often does, on hyperbole, Jesus even forbids the use of titles at all (though it does seem titles, of a sort, were used in the early church). *God* is the Father. *Jesus* is the teacher. The church is a *family*. And the most powerful person in the house is the one who volunteers to *scrub toilets*. This is Jesus' alternative vision for religious community and religious leadership. It remains his challenge for us even today.

Eugene Peterson, translator of *The Message* and pastor to one church for twenty-nine years, used to say that the Christian message is subversive. We don't defeat the world by going toe to toe, using worldly weapons in the service of God. Rather, we undermine the world by living quiet lives of repentance and faith. The gospel subverts the powers of the world by dismissing them as mere foolishness, by shrugging them off the way Jesus shrugged off Herod Antipas ("that fox"). And in these days of revived paganism on both the right and the left—where carnal power is a virtue and self-effacing humility is once again viewed as a vice (as it was to the ancient Greeks and Romans)—perhaps the gospel nowhere undermines the world better than in its vision of leadership, where getting to be "in charge" is never the point, where greatest among us is the one who serves, and where the king of the world is the one who carried a cross.

May we all, beginning with myself, be people who are shaped by that cross. And may the world find in *that* a challenge it doesn't know how to face.

Let's Pray

12.

Divine Healing

ADVENT WEEK 1

1 *One day Peter and John were going up to the temple at the time of prayer—at three in the afternoon.* **2** *Now a man who was lame from birth was being carried to the temple gate called Beautiful, where he was put every day to beg from those going into the temple courts.* **3** *When he saw Peter and John about to enter, he asked them for money.* **4** *Peter looked straight at him, as did John. Then Peter said, "Look at us!"* **5** *So the man gave them his attention, expecting to get something from them.*

6 *Then Peter said, "Silver or gold I do not have, but what I do have I give you. In the name of Jesus Christ of Nazareth, walk."* **7** *Taking him by the right hand, he helped him up, and instantly the man's feet and ankles became strong.* **8** *He jumped to his feet and began to walk. Then he went with them into the temple courts, walking and jumping, and praising God.* **9** *When all the people saw him walking and praising God,* **10** *they recognized him as the same man who used to sit begging at the temple gate*

A BASIS OF FELLOWSHIP

called Beautiful, and they were filled with wonder and amazement at what had happened to him.

Acts 3:1–10

THIS MORNING BEGINS OUR Advent journey toward Christmas. Outside the walls of the church, it's shopping season. Thanksgiving has come and gone. So have the Black Friday sales. Now we enter that time when nostalgia and cynicism both get dialed to 11. But inside the church, we've entered the season of waiting. Instead of looking back, we look forward. And instead of being cynical, we hope.

Our topic today is the doctrine of divine healing, which is a complicated topic at best. Wide is the path of destruction Christians have left in their desire to see miracles happen: people told to stop taking their medicine because they've been healed, only to wind up getting worse instead of better; others told they are sick because they don't have enough faith, that their illness and suffering are essentially their fault (though it's usually said a bit more kindly than that). But wide also is the path trod by those who claim to have seen the miraculous, to have seen someone healed or been healed themselves. For every Christian who denies that miraculous healings take place today, there is another who has had it happen in their own life. And for every Christian who insists we all can experience healing right now, there is another whose faithful prayers have gone unanswered for years. Sometimes it feels cruel to pray for someone's healing, knowing it very well may not happen, and we feel we should probably instead pray for comfort. But on the other hand, if God does in fact heal—even sometimes—how cruel would it be to pray for comfort but not pray for healing?

The twelfth fundamental truth of the Assemblies of God is on divine healing, and it reads like this:

> *"Divine healing is an integral part of the gospel. Deliverance from sickness is provided for in the Atonement, and is the privilege of all believers."*

The confidence with which this fundamental truth is worded is admittedly a challenge for me. I was raised by a chronically ill mother who loved Jesus as much as anybody I know. From the time she was in middle school, she had regular seizures. As an adult, her doctor didn't think she should have children, and when she became pregnant with my older brother, he insisted on aborting the baby. She and my father refused, and after a long search, they found someone who would do the delivery in spite of the risks. My brother was born happy and healthy. Four years later, I was born. This second pregnancy and delivery did not go as well, and after I was born, my mother's health got much worse. I remember, as a child, my mother being medicated nearly out of her mind in hopes of curbing her seizures. It never worked. Eventually, when I was in fifth grade, doctors discovered a brain tumor and removed it. After a year or so, her seizures finally stopped. Fifteen years later, she got cancer. Faithful women prayed with her and for her to be healed. Once she even believed she was healed and went to her next doctor's appointment fully convinced. When the appointment revealed nothing unusual, that her cancer was still there and responding as expected to treatment, she came home devastated. Due to complications related to the cancer, my mother eventually died.

On the other hand, I know three people, including my wife, whose healings from cancer (or apparent cancer) are so unusual as to demand an unusual explanation. In the case of all three, prayer was integral to the recovery process. For my wife, in her childhood, the illness that had her hospitalized one day, and was believed to be leukemia pending further testing, was gone the next, with the only intervening factor being a nighttime visit for prayer from an uncle who was an Assemblies of God minister. It's a story that could be easily dismissed as a series of coincidences and medical misdiagnoses. But for my wife and I, we believe she experienced a miracle. Divine healing, as far as I can see, is both as simple as our statement of faith claims it to be, and as complicated as human experience.

A BASIS OF FELLOWSHIP

In our passage this morning, two of Jesus' disciples are on their way to temple to pray. This is after the death and resurrection of Jesus, and after his ascension into heaven and the pouring out of the Holy Spirit on the church. As these two men get close to the Temple, they are greeted by a beggar asking for help. The man has been lame from birth, chronically disabled (we are told later) for over forty years. He is hoping for some money, but the disciples don't have any. Instead of money, says Peter, what they have is the name of Jesus. So in that name Peter commands the man to be healed, grabs his hand, and pulls him to his feet. It's the sort of scene we'd all be horrified to witness in church, except for the fact that it actually works. The man's feet and ankles grow instantly strong, and by the time Peter has him on his feet, he can stand for the first time in his life. He immediately begins jumping and praising God and accompanies the disciples into the Temple, where he quickly draws a crowd. The worshipers, who have passed this man for years every time they've gone to temple, immediately recognize him. Wonder and amazement fills the crowd. And Peter very wisely uses the opportunity to share the gospel.

Protestant Christians have a long history of both affirming that miracles like this took place in the Bible and also denying that they happen in the modern day church. It's an easy position to take because it accords with both Scripture and experience. The Bible says it happened back then, so I believe it. But also, I've never seen a miracle (we might say), so I also don't believe they happen right now. It's a position that had its start in conflict with Roman Catholics during the Protestant Reformation. The Catholic Church claimed many miracles, and therefore used the absence of miracles among Protestants as proof they had walked away from God. "We have our Bibles," was the Protestant response, "you can take your miracles and shove 'em."

But ever since the rise of the Pentecostal and charismatic movements in the church, among both Protestants and Catholics, the claim that miracles no longer take place has become harder to defend. By one estimate, the number of Christians who have claimed to experience divine healing in the modern world exceeds

200 million people. This estimate excludes the church in China, which itself numbers in the millions despite persecution, and where the China Christian Council estimates nearly fifty percent of conversions have taken place due to witnessing, or personally experiencing, a miraculous healing. Almost three-quarters of medical doctors in the United States admit to believing in miracles, and over half of those responding to one survey claimed to have seen one themselves.

Clearly, however, not everyone is healed. Healings do take place in Europe and the United States, but not nearly so often as in the developing world. One could, in an unconscious moment of racism, explain this by saying the people of the Majority World (or "Third World") aren't as sophisticated as us Westerners. They're superstitious and gullible, while we are skeptical and scientific. But perhaps a better explanation is our relative wealth versus their relative poverty. "Silver and gold I do not have," said Peter. Silver and gold we have aplenty, even if our assumptions about what constitutes "comfortable living" makes us feel like we don't. We have so much more to rely on in times of need than people in the Majority World often do. Also, while we tend to pursue healing for a whole number of reasons, the healing of the man in our passage appears to have been granted by God for the sake of bearing witness to the gospel. And we also, as a culture, tend to think of suffering as an abnormality, while most cultures (both historically and right now) accept suffering as a part of life. This man's healing led to a gospel opportunity, but it also led to the first persecution of the church. How often would we pray for healing if we knew we would receive a beating for it later? How much more likely would God answer our prayers if we cared about the person we were praying for so much, and God's glory so much, that we really didn't care what happened to us after the prayer? What if praying for someone's healing was almost guaranteed to cost us our life?

Our statement of faith says healing is the privilege of every believer, and perhaps some of what I've said sounds like I don't believe this is true. But I do. This is the first Sunday of Advent, after all, the time for waiting and hope. And I believe Advent puts this entire discussion of healing into proper perspective.

Advent is the time of waiting. We enter, through our imaginations, into the waiting of Israel for the coming of Christ. Advent is also our reminder that Christ will come again. It is the reminder that we, too, wait and hope. In our American culture, Advent and Christmas experience a strange overlap. We light Advent candles, but we've also already decorated our tree. As *Americans*, Christmas feels like it's already (a little bit, at least) here. But as *Christians* we know Christmas isn't here yet. It's already here, but also not yet. The same goes for the kingdom of God and the salvation and healing that it brings.

The world *will* one day be healed. All causes of sickness and death will one day be gone. Our bodies, in that day, will rise like Christ's glorified body, and then every one of us will be healed. Our healing will have been won for us at the cross (as our statement of faith says), and this will have been brought to effect by God's Holy Spirit.

In the meantime, as we live in the "already but not yet" of the kingdom of God, the challenge remains for us to believe in the God who does miracles. We aren't "off the hook" when it comes to praying for the healing of others. The challenge remains for us to love, serve, and (above all, if we really believe in God) *pray* for those who suffer, to love even our enemies, and to share the good news of Jesus every opportunity we have. The challenge remains for us to enter the tension of hope-filled suffering, of joy in the midst of pain, of patience and gratitude, which is the historic experience of all God's people, both Old Testament and New. This is the tension of Christian existence, and this is the meaning of Advent.

Let's Pray

13.

The Blessed Hope (The Rapture of the Church)

ADVENT WEEK 2

13 *Brothers and sisters, we do not want you to be uninformed about those who sleep in death, so that you do not grieve like the rest of mankind, who have no hope.* **14** *For we believe that Jesus died and rose again, and so we believe that God will bring with Jesus those who have fallen asleep in him.* **15** *According to the Lord's word, we tell you that we who are still alive, who are left until the coming of the Lord, will certainly not precede those who have fallen asleep.* **16** *For the Lord himself will come down from heaven, with a loud command, with the voice of the archangel and with the trumpet call of God, and the dead in Christ will rise first.* **17** *After that, we who are still alive and are left will be caught up together with them in the clouds to meet the Lord in the air. And so we will be with the Lord forever.* **18** *Therefore encourage one another with these words.*

1 Thessalonians 4:13–18

THIS MORNING BEGINS THE second week of Advent. We are now a full week into the Christian year and one week closer to the coming of Christ, both symbolically and literally. Christmas is closer this Sunday than it was last Sunday, and the return of Christ for his church is one week closer than it was a week ago. Through the imaginative traditions of Advent and Christmas, and through the literal and Scripture-built hopes of the church, our eyes are looking for Jesus. He's almost here.

The Advent theme for last Sunday, which we touched on indirectly through the topic of healing, was *hope*. The theme for this second Sunday of Advent is *peace*. But how often do we, as Christians, relate the second coming of Jesus with peace? A common theme I hear from people about my age who grew up in the evangelical or Pentecostal church is a childhood fear of missing the rapture. For some, this fear was so acute it kept them awake at night. Horrifying images of the Antichrist, the Mark of the Beast, and the Great Tribulation filled their heads. Were they ready? Did they really believe? Have they been making sure to confess all known sin? Their childhoods sound pretty frightening to me. Not surprisingly, most of the folks I hear this from have either left the church altogether or at least have found a theology that doesn't scare them as much. One can only live at an emotional fever pitch for so long. But when I turn to my New Testament to see what it has to say about Jesus coming back, what I see there is hope and not fear. Of course, there are frightening images, too. The world can be a scary place, and judgment on evil is incumbent upon God. But when Jesus tells his disciples, "I go to prepare a place for you," he doesn't follow it up with, "so be very afraid." The world is filled with trouble, but Jesus has overcome the world and gives us his peace.

The thirteenth fundamental truth in our statement of faith is titled "The Blessed Hope," and it reads like this:

> "The resurrection of those who have fallen asleep in Christ and their translation together with those who are alive and remain uno the coming of the Lord is the imminent and blessed hope of the Church."

THE BLESSED HOPE (THE RAPTURE OF THE CHURCH)

The language for this statement comes from the passage we've just read in 1 Thessalonians. Here Paul is answering the question, "What happens to believers who die before Jesus comes back?" and his answer is that they are safe with God and will come back with Jesus when Jesus returns for his church.

"Brothers and sisters," Paul says, "we do not want you to be uninformed about those who sleep in death." Nor does he want them to mourn for their dead in the hopeless way of unbelievers. Christ has risen from death and conquered it. The death of our loved ones is, therefore, not the final word. Those who died in faith are in the presence of God. When Christ returns for his church, they will return with him. And just as Christ rose bodily from the grave, so will their souls reunite with their bodies and the dead in Christ will rise first. Then we, too, who are alive in that moment will be caught up with them, transformed "in the twinkling of an eye," as Paul says in 1 Corinthians 15:52. We will meet Christ in the air and will be with him forever. "Therefore," says Paul, "encourage one another with these words."

There are other details, too, of course. If we keep reading past our text, we will see that the rapture of the church means tribulation for the world. Those who refuse to separate themselves from the darkness will be consumed along with it. But Paul doesn't say these things with an eye toward frightening believers. He says it all for their, and for our, encouragement. Whether the rapture of the church and Christ's second coming to earth are distinct events or happen all at once, the return of Christ is something for which Paul wants believers to yearn. Like the apostle Peter, when Jesus called him out of the boat to walk on the water, everything depends on where our focus lies. Are we looking at the waves of current events and end times theories—are we looking, even, at the frightening images we see in our Bibles—or are we looking at Jesus, the one who is coming to save us? Is our focus the scary things that might happen between now and the end? Or is it the redemption of our bodies and life everlasting?

The Jesus who is coming for his church is the Prince of Peace, just as the baby born on Christmas was and is the Mighty God. To believe in Jesus is to believe we are in a story that is going somewhere, a story that is both frightening and beautiful. When we are most tempted to be sentimental and saccharine, the Bible challenges us with difficult words. And when we are most inclined to be anxious, the God of the Bible says, "Do not be afraid." Thinking about the Second Coming might feel worlds away from twinkling lights and Christmas trees, but our text and those lights are both pointing the same way. They point us to the Christ who has come and is coming again. They point us to the hope of the church.

Let's Pray

14.

The Millennial Reign of Christ

ADVENT WEEK 3

1 And I saw an angel coming down out of heaven, having the key to the Abyss and holding in his hand a great chain. 2 He seized the dragon, that ancient serpent, who is the devil, or Satan, and bound him for a thousand years. 3 He threw him into the Abyss, and locked and sealed it over him, to keep him from deceiving the nations anymore until the thousand years were ended. After that, he must be set free for a short time.

4 I saw thrones on which were seated those who had been given authority to judge. And I saw the souls of those who had been beheaded because of their testimony about Jesus and because of the word of God. They[a] had not worshiped the beast or its image and had not received its mark on their foreheads or their hands. They came to life and reigned with Christ a thousand years. 5 (The rest of the dead did not come to life until the thousand years were ended.) This is the first resurrection. 6 Blessed and holy are those who share in the first resurrection. The second death has no power over them, but they will be

A BASIS OF FELLOWSHIP

priests of God and of Christ and will reign with him for a thousand years.

Revelation 20:1–6

8 *And there were shepherds living out in the fields nearby, keeping watch over their flocks at night.* **9** *An angel of the Lord appeared to them, and the glory of the Lord shone around them, and they were terrified.* **10** *But the angel said to them, "Do not be afraid. I bring you good news that will cause great joy for all the people.* **11** *Today in the town of David a Savior has been born to you; he is the Messiah, the Lord.* **12** *This will be a sign to you: You will find a baby wrapped in cloths and lying in a manger."*

13 *Suddenly a great company of the heavenly host appeared with the angel, praising God and saying,*

14 *"Glory to God in the highest heaven,
and on earth peace to those on whom his favor rests."*

Luke 2:8–14

"Peace on earth." It's not a phrase you hear people say very often anymore, but it was once one of the most common refrains you would hear around Christmas time. "Peace on earth, goodwill toward men." It was a paraphrase of the angels' words in Luke chapter 2, and it was part of the theme of every Christmas season.

On July 28, 1914, one month after the assassination of Archduke Francis Ferdinand, the Austro-Hungarian Empire declared war on Serbia, launching Europe into World War One, the bloodiest war in human history up to that point. In the span of four years, approximately 22 million people would die. A combination of outdated thinking and high-tech weaponry meant that every battle was a slaughter. Tens of thousands of men would die in every charge, mowed down by machine guns and crushed by tanks. It was the "war to end all wars," people said. Two decades later, however, an even bloodier war would begin, covering even more of the planet and resulting in twice the number of dead. But five

THE MILLENNIAL REIGN OF CHRIST

months into that First World War, before hearts had become too bitter from the violence and officers had issued too many commands to the contrary, there was a series of events that came to be known as the Christmas Truce.

In November and December of 1914, but especially leading up to Christmas Eve and Christmas Day, German and British solders began talking to each other across the No Man's Land between their trenches. Many Germans knew English, and no one on either side really wanted to fight. Soldiers on both sides would agree to take breaks from the shooting so people could gather their dead. If one side had just been issued their rations, or had some sort of menial work to do like digging, the other side agreed to give them a break for at least half an hour. Germans who had gone to school in London asked their British enemies for football scores. And as the Christmas holiday approached, men whose job it was to murder each other began joining each other in song, cigarettes, and impromptu games of soccer.

This truce, of course, wouldn't last. And it wasn't universal. Some soldiers, in their letters, related hearing shooting to the right and left while their own section of the front shared cigarettes and newspapers with the enemy. Officers on both sides objected to this peaceful behavior among their men, most famously a German lance corporal named Adolf Hitler. And by the end of the war, both sides hated each other so much no one was interested in such a truce. But for a few brief moments in 1914, men chose to lay down their arms and stop killing each other. They did it for many beautiful and funny reasons. One of the reasons they did it was simply because it was Christmas. "Peace on earth, goodwill toward men."

The fourteenth fundamental truth, titled "The Millennial Reign of Christ," reads like this:

> *"The second coming of Christ includes the rapture of the saints, which is our blessed hope, followed by the visible return of Christ with His saints to reign on the earth for one thousand years. This millennial reign will bring the*

> *salvation of national Israel and the establishment of universal peace."*

At least since the days of Saint Augustine, this millennial reign of Christ on the earth has been interpreted to mean that Christ rules on earth through the church. But earlier generations of Christians, including some directly discipled by the apostle John, looked forward to a future day of sabbath rest for this earth. They looked forward to a millennium, a thousand years of peace that Christ would bring when he returned. They looked forward to a day when the lion would eat grass like the ox, when the wolf would live with the lamb, the leopard would lie down with the goat, the calf and the lion and the yearling together, and a little child would lead them. Just as God had commanded a sabbath day and a sabbath year for his people Israel, so he would grant a sabbath rest to the whole earth before a cosmic "eighth day," the day of universal resurrection, judgment, and new creation.

It seems hard to look out on the world right now and believe God is going to bring peace to this place. Every human peace, like the Christmas truce of 1914, gets swallowed up by an even more gruesome season of war. Even the millennium, if we understand the book of Revelation rightly, will be followed by a final time of testing in which many will once again show their evil sides. But the God of the Bible is a God of peace, just as he is also at times a God of war. He will one day crush evil. He will one day cry out to the armies of the world, "Be still!" He will send his Son to defeat every enemy of God, the final enemy of God being death itself. He will prepare this world for the new creation. He will rule the earth with peace.

Let's Pray

15.

The Final Judgment

ADVENT WEEK 4

16 For God so loved the world that he gave his one and only Son, that whoever believes in him shall not perish but have eternal life. 17 For God did not send his Son into the world to condemn the world, but to save the world through him. 18 Whoever believes in him is not condemned, but whoever does not believe stands condemned already because they have not believed in the name of God's one and only Son. 19 This is the verdict: Light has come into the world, but people loved darkness instead of light because their deeds were evil. 20 Everyone who does evil hates the light, and will not come into the light for fear that their deeds will be exposed. 21 But whoever lives by the truth comes into the light, so that it may be seen plainly that what they have done has been done in the sight of God.

John 3:16–21

THE SUNDAY BEFORE CHRISTMAS feels like a strange time to talk about Judgment Day—especially when we realize the theme for this fourth Sunday of Advent is *love*.

A BASIS OF FELLOWSHIP

The idea that God judges can feel like the furthest thing from the idea that God loves. And there is (perhaps) a tension between judgment and love. But to paraphrase one author who spent his childhood surrounded by war and ethnic violence, you have to live a pretty charmed life to think a God who never judges is the God we really need. After all, how loving is a God who never does anything about evil? Who looks the other way when injustice takes place? How loving would God be if he refused to set all that is wrong in this world finally right? Even people who don't believe in God get upset at God for allowing so much evil in the world. That God has given humanity the dangerous freedom of genuine choice is one thing. If God never went on to hold us accountable for those choices, that would be another thing entirely.

The fifteenth fundamental truth of the Assemblies of God opens with the ominous phrase, *"There will be a final judgment. . ."* The focus of this next-to-last fundamental truth is on the condemnation of the wicked, on every person whose name *"is not found written in the Book of Life."* It's sobering and terrifying. To a suffering church under persecution, it's also probably comforting. Not only are the unbelieving judged, but so is antichrist, false religion, and the devil himself. Using the language of the white throne judgment in Revelation chapter 20, our statement of faith pictures a day when wickedness is finally gathered together before God and dealt with once for all, thus making way for God's new creation.

In our passage this morning, we come across what may be the most famous verse in all the Bible: "For God so loved the world that he gave his one and only Son, that whoever believes in him shall not perish but have eternal life." The context of this verse is Jesus' conversation with the religious leader Nicodemus. It's the famous "you must be born again" conversation we looked at a couple months ago when we thought about the doctrine of salvation. A religious leader comes to Jesus under the cover of darkness. He's there at night because he doesn't want to be seen by his colleagues or gossiped about by the crowds. He wants to have a conversation with Jesus.

THE FINAL JUDGMENT

Over the course of the conversation between Jesus and Nicodemus, Nicodemus admits that he and his fellow religious leaders know Jesus has been sent by God. They know his miracles are genuine. What they don't know is what to do with him. Jesus is a threat to their power, their influence, and their way of life. He regularly undermines much of their teaching and he not infrequently points out their hypocrisy. They know he is from God, but they don't like him. Nicodemus, too, knows Jesus is from God. But instead of viewing Jesus as an enemy, Nicodemus wants to talk.

Jesus, however, doesn't seem interested in these introductory remarks. He (by all appearances) changes the subject and tells Nicodemus that he, Nicodemus, needs to be "born again." Nicodemus doesn't know what Jesus means, but Jesus keeps pressing the point. What Nicodemus needs isn't more of what Nicodemus already has. No. Nicodemus needs a hard reset. He needs a new beginning. He must be born again. Then Jesus goes on to predict his (Jesus') own death on the cross and tells Nicodemus that the eternal life Nicodemus seeks will come to him by trusting in Jesus.

It's a whirlwind of a conversation, and our passage this morning is the apostle John's commentary on it (though some scholars and translators treat these verses as still being a quote by Jesus). God loves the world, says John, and he has loved the world in a particular way: by sending his Son to die on the cross. The reason God sent Jesus into the world wasn't so God could finally condemn the world. Jesus didn't show up just to tell people what sinners they all are. Rather, God sent his Son for the purpose of redemption. Those who trust in this Son find the life of heaven taking up residence in their hearts. They find themselves standing in light, loving the light, and wanting to be filled more and more with that light. Those who don't trust in this Son (who, like Nicodemus' colleagues, may even have a high view of Jesus, but still think of him more as a threat than a Savior) find themselves condemned, not merely for rejecting God's Son, but for rejecting their own second chance. They are already condemned for the ways they have lived, the words they have said, the things they have done. And perhaps most importantly, the things they have *not* done. They love darkness (like the darkness Nicodemus is standing in) even though God is offering them light.

The idea of judgment often bothers us because we don't believe we deserve to be judged. The wrongs done by others anger us to our core, but our own wrongs have a "good explanation." When others mock or insult us, we feel the sting of their words. But when we do the same to someone else, we demand to be pardoned because what we said was "just a joke" or we were "just saying it like it is." Like Nicodemus' colleagues, we have a particular love affair with the dark. We know light is good, as long as it shines where we want it to shine. But if it gets too close to those things we want kept in the dark, then the light (which we know is good) becomes a threat. We run from it. We hide from it. We set up walls in our lives to keep it out. We want to be anywhere, with anyone, doing anything, as long as we're not in that light.

On the other hand, sometimes our struggle with the idea of judgment is because we are only too aware of how much we deserve it. We know we have done wrong. We know we have often avoided what's right. We know that even if our actions don't betray us, the secret thoughts of our hearts surely do. Our struggle, in this case, is less with the idea that we are guilty as it is with the question whether God could ever forgive us.

To both of these reactions to God's word of judgment, the Bible's counsel is: welcome it. Welcome God's judgment. The light is coming, and the best thing we can do is step into that light. For those of us who covet our sin, Jesus says, "Step into the light." Stop loving the darkness. Stop saying your sin isn't so bad. You know that God condemns your sin, so let him. Look to the cross and let God say "No" to your sin. Let the death of Christ be your death. Let the punishment that fell upon innocent Jesus be your punishment. Let it be peace between you and God, and fall out of love with your sin.

And for those who fear God's judgment because you know you don't measure up: You also need to welcome God's judgment. You also need to step into the light. Let God's painful light shine on your sin, and know that through the cross of Christ you, too, can be forgiven. "For God did not send his Son into the world to condemned the world, but to save it."

The one thing we do not want to do is to run from the light, because we cannot run forever. And when the darkness finally passes, and there is nowhere left to hide, all that is left will be light.

Let's Pray

16.

The New Heavens and Earth

FIRST SUNDAY AFTER CHRISTMAS DAY

> 1 Then I saw "a new heaven and a new earth," for the first heaven and the first earth had passed away, and there was no longer any sea. 2 I saw the Holy City, the new Jerusalem, coming down out of heaven from God, prepared as a bride beautifully dressed for her husband. 3 And I heard a loud voice from the throne saying, "Look! God's dwelling place is now among the people, and he will dwell with them. They will be his people, and God himself will be with them and be their God. 4 'He will wipe every tear from their eyes. There will be no more death' or mourning or crying or pain, for the old order of things has passed away."
>
> Revelation 21:1–4

WELL, WE FINALLY MADE it. It's the first Sunday after Christmas and the last Sunday of the year. We're now in that weird limbo between Christmas Day and New Year's Eve. A chronological no-man's-land. It sort of feels like 2024 is over, but it's also not yet 2025. It *is* technically still Christmas, of course, at least until we arrive at Epiphany on January 6th.

THE NEW HEAVENS AND EARTH

You'll notice we sang Christmas songs again this morning. These twelve days between Christmas and Epiphany are what give us the "Twelve Days of Christmas" from the famous song with all its weird gifts. But in my family—like the good non-liturgical, American Christians we are—when my daughter's aunt gave her a Christmas gift with twelve compartments, one for each day of Christmas, all of us called it an Advent calendar and timed things so Ava would open the last compartment Christmas Eve. Every person, family, and culture does things differently, of course. But for us, everything is about that run-up to Christmas Day. Once the calendar turns to December 26th, even if we aren't done Christmas-ing quite yet (we're having dinner with my brother and sister-in-law this afternoon, in fact), it still sort of feels like the boat has left the dock. We haven't kicked on the engine quite yet, so we're drifting. It's peaceful and a little melancholy. I don't know whether to look at New Year's Eve—when we pull the cord and fire up the engine—as an exciting moment or an interruption to the peace and quiet. In reality, of course, it's sort of both. But for now, the engine is off, it's not New Year's yet, and we are just floating along.

The sixteenth and final fundamental truth is titled "The New Heavens and the New Earth," and it is simply a quote of 2 Peter 3:13 in the King James Version: *"We, according to His promise, look for new heavens and a new earth, wherein dwelleth righteousness."*

I've intentionally avoided going chronologically through the final chapters of Revelation as we've gone through these final doctrinal points. I think Revelation makes our brains shut down after a while. The imagery is so intense, and we've been trained to notice the fire and the brimstone, the antichrist and the plagues, more than we have been trained to see God in this book. Also, I've wanted to spark people's spiritual imaginations a bit, which strangely enough doesn't always happen when we read Revelation. For Revelation's mysterious thousand year reign, I had no choice but to come to this book. On the issue of the rapture, I actually *had* to go somewhere else, and on the issue of judgment, I chose to go to the Gospel of John.

There are other places I could have gone to discuss the re-creation of heaven and earth, too, of course. But there are few portions in Scripture more beautiful than these final two chapters of Revelation. Even though these chapters, too, contain sober warnings, the warp and woof of this portion of text is beauty, healing, redemption, and arrival. The warnings are there simply to say, "You don't want to miss this!" Revelation 21 and 22 are where the book has been going the whole time. And in the opening of John's final vision, which happens to be our text this morning, the book of Revelation finally *arrives*.

On this final Sunday of the year, as we look back to 2024 and forward to 2025, let's remember that the Bible is much more about beginnings than endings. Every person in Christ, no matter how old they are, has more future in front of them than past behind them. And while we in the pastor business tend to call these final doctrinal points "eschatology" (meaning "doctrines about the end"), this final topic and text are really the prologue to a whole new book that hasn't yet been written (except, of course, in the mind of God).

Revelation 21 and 22 are like the last Sunday of the year. It's sort of not Christmas anymore (even though it still kind of is), but it's also not next year yet, either. John has a vision of how that ultimate New Year will start. But after he sees heaven and earth come together and the nations walk into God's holy city, the book closes with invitations and warnings and then the end credits roll. The Bible leaves us looking at the next creation, knowing it will come, knowing it will bring healing, and knowing almost nothing beyond that. All we know is that God will be there. And, if we have embraced Christ as our Savior, we will be there, too.

> 1 *Then the angel showed me the river of the water of life, as clear as crystal, flowing from the throne of God and of the Lamb* 2 *down the middle of the great street of the city. On each side of the river stood the tree of life, bearing twelve crops of fruit, yielding its fruit every month. And the leaves of the tree are for the healing of the nations.* 3 *No longer will there be any curse. The throne of God and of the Lamb*

will be in the city, and his servants will serve him. 4 *They will see his face, and his name will be on their foreheads.* 5 *There will be no more night. They will not need the light of a lamp or the light of the sun, for the Lord God will give them light. And they will reign for ever and ever.*

Revelation 22:1–5

Let's Pray

www.ingramcontent.com/pod-product-compliance
Lightning Source LLC
Chambersburg PA
CBHW071743090426
42738CB00011B/2540